# Everything You Always Wanted to Know About Fly Fishing

# Everything You Always Wanted to Know About Fly Fishing

### Patrick Straub

### All Expert Advice Portraits by Austin Trayser

LYONS PRESS
Guilford, Connecticut
*An imprint of Globe Pequot Press*

Lyons Press is an imprint of Globe Pequot Press.

Project editor: Staci Zacharski
Text design and layout artist: Sue Murray
All expert advice portraits by Austin Trayser

Library of Congress Cataloging-in-Publication Data

Straub, Patrick.
  Everything you always wanted to know about fly fishing-- but were afraid to ask /
Patrick Straub.
     pages cm
  Includes index.
  ISBN 978-0-7627-7391-6
  1. Fly fishing. I. Title.
  SH456.S825 2013
  799.12'4--dc23
                                    2013019007

Printed in the United States of America

10 9 8 7 6 5 4 3 2 1

# CONTENTS

# ACKNOWLEDGMENTS

So many people played a large part in the creation of this book. To list them all would be cause for another book. However, as with any project there are a special few who deserve to stand out in a crowd.

First, thanks to Allen Jones, my patient and tireless editor. His work and dedication is greatly appreciated but never fully acknowledged. Thanks to Chris Dombrowski. Angler. Friend. Poet. Troutslayer. Thanks to all of the fishing clients and friends I have been with over the years—Jeff Shrader, Paul Meripol, Page McCoy, John Marmaduke, John Rutherford, and many others.

Gratitude is deserved for the personalities in this book who allowed me into their homes or shops to interview them and pick their brain.

Thanks to my family for allowing me to fish as much as I did, and still do.

Most importantly, thanks to my wife, Brandy Moses Straub. She understands my passion, and for that I am eternally thankful.

# HOW TO USE THIS BOOK

Fly fishing is the perfect pastime. It's easy to learn. Damn near impossible to master, yet provides enough reward to keep you coming back. *Everything You Always Wanted to Know About Fly Fishing* is for any angler who's enjoyed fly fishing. It's also for any angler who wishes to become a better angler; a better steward of the river; or just needs something to read to get them through the winter.

This book originally started as a collection of my thoughts and advice. As I got into the manuscript more and more, I realized much of what I learned came from other anglers—other anglers who'd been doing it a lot longer than I. The book needed more.

So I went out and got more . . . I sat down with some of those anglers, outfitters, guides, and mentors who helped me grow as an angler and a guide, for without them my growth as angler would have taken that much longer. Fortunately, you have this book. I wanted the instruction to be real. I wanted you, the reader, to feel as if you were in the room with us. These interviews offer personal, first-hand experience with greatness—greatness that I alone could never come close to offering as the author of a book claiming to know everything.

Granted, I've fished a ton and fished in a lot of amazing places. However, in my desire to give to you *Everything You Always Wanted to Know About Fly Fishing,* there were still some things I needed to ask!

My introduction to fly fishing occurred late during the month of May on the Yellowstone River. It was a brazen attempt to feel success in something that, at the time, I had no idea would be a lifelong learning process and passion. Growing up in the Gallatin and Paradise Valleys, I was a rambunctious teenager who cared more about which girls might be calling me tonight rather than appreciating the mountains, trees, and rivers that framed my life, as well as the view from my bedroom window.

On that first day, the entire experience scripted like a Hollywood movie with us cast as the townies, or "cutters"—my buddies and I skipped our afternoon classes at Bozeman High School, loaded into a two-wheel-drive Chevy Luv pickup, and we arrived at the Yellowstone River dressed for angling success in our cutoffs and plaid flannel shirts. For us it didn't really matter that the river was high, muddy, and carried the occasional tree, bobbing down in the high water, from somewhere in Yellowstone National Park. The drama of the fast and loud currents and our inability to cast a line farther than an empty beer can could be tossed made it even more heart-thumping. Seeing my fly drift down the current of a river, even if it floated under my nose, was enough for me. Too bad such low expectations couldn't always hold my interest.

The more I fished the more I realized I knew less and less about fly fishing, rivers, and trout. But that intrigued me, and the more time I spent fishing rivers in Montana, the more I learned about myself, my relationships with others, and how I felt about conservation.

After high school and in college, I searched out every "how-to," "where-to," and "why-do" fly-fishing books I could find. During runoff I would peruse the used bookstores looking for books new to me. In winter I would re-read my favorite books and watch the weather, and on any day warmer than 30 degrees, I would be on a river while my buddies were skiing.

I learned to fly fish entirely on my own through trial and error. Yes, I had a thirty-minute casting lesson here and there, and was drug along by my older brother out of obligation, but for the most part I spent hours untangling line from the bushes in the meadows of Slough Creek, lost nearly a year's tuition in flies to the willows of the Yellowstone, and my IRA is in flies left in the lips of Missouri rainbows.

These days I have made fishing and writing my lifestyle, and feel extremely lucky to have carved out a wonderful niche for myself. After guiding and outfitting for over a decade now, I feel there are lots of questions that anglers of all abilities still look to have answered. Plus the style of how information is presented these days can be as dry as a Wyoming dirt road in August.

I honestly feel like the "how-to" guidebook market is saturated. However, I did not want to bore readers with the same "how-to" format, plus I wanted one book to have several different approaches to the various "hows" of fly fishing and have a book that beginning, intermediate, and highly skilled anglers would all benefit from reading. Out of those thoughts came the idea for this book and then the subsequent interviews.

The format of the book is simple: questions and answers that I have created and interviews I had with some great angling personalities. I've highlighted some of the major points for easy reference. Plus it is not essential to read the book cover-to-cover, in that order. Please feel free to skip around and read what peaks your interest first, but rest assured you will learn something from this book—even if you think you know it all.

# Chapter One

# Instant Gratification

## Be a Better Angler Right Now.
## Improve Immediately

### What's the difference between fly fishing and spin casting?

Think back to your days as a spin fisherman, if there were any. Remember what happened when you tried to cast too light of a lure with your spinning rod, say, a $\frac{1}{16}$-ounce jig on 12-pound test? Even with the wind at your back, you couldn't cast 10 feet—the lure was simply too light to flex the rod and pull the line off the reel, and the line likely tangled as a result. But if you switched the $\frac{1}{16}$-ounce jig to something like a $\frac{3}{4}$-ounce jig, your cast would zing out across the lake. In spin-fishing, it's the weight of the lure that loads the rod and propels a fairly weightless monofilament line through the air.

However, in fly fishing, dry-fly fishing at least, the inverse process is at work: The weight of the synthetic fly line loads the rod and propels a fairly weightless fly through the air. A standard, 9-foot, five-weight rod, for instance, will be matched and loaded with a 5- or 6-weight line, a line that is heavy enough to load (read: flex) the rod but not so heavy that the rod gets overloaded, flexed beyond its means. Additionally, a 3- or 4-weight line will not provide enough weight to properly load the rod, and the angler attempting to cast such a combo will find himself in the same position as the spin fisherman mentioned above—pretty much powerless.

If you've spin-fished for years, transitioning to fly fishing, with its new world of gear and terminology, might seem like too great an undertaking, but for myriad reasons the switch can be a very rewarding one.

### Why should I consider fly fishing over other ways of catching fish?

What are the potential rewards? For starters, under most conditions on Western rivers, a good fly angler will catch as many or more fish than a good spin fisher, since fly anglers can more easily imitate the appearance and behavior of aquatic insects (caddis, mayflies, and stoneflies) that make up the bulk of a trout's diet. During periods of intense bug activity (be this a caddis emergence, blanket mayfly spinner fall, or egg-laying flight of stoneflies), the spin fisher chucking lures will be unable to draw fish away from their dominant food source, whereas the fly angler can provide a near-exact match of what dominates the food line.

Sure, a Mepps spinner might fool one fish out of a rising pod of picky trout feeding on tiny mayflies on the Clark Fork River in late September, but the fly angler offering a more prudent imitation of the small, grayish mayfly will catch half a dozen.

And, numbers aside, casting a fly rod is just more fun than chunking and winding.

### How do I cast efficiently?

Casting a fly rod effectively depends first and foremost on the caster's understanding of rhythm and timing. The standard cast is often described as a two-part act: the backcast, and then the forward cast. I prefer to say that the fly cast is a three-part act: the backcast, followed

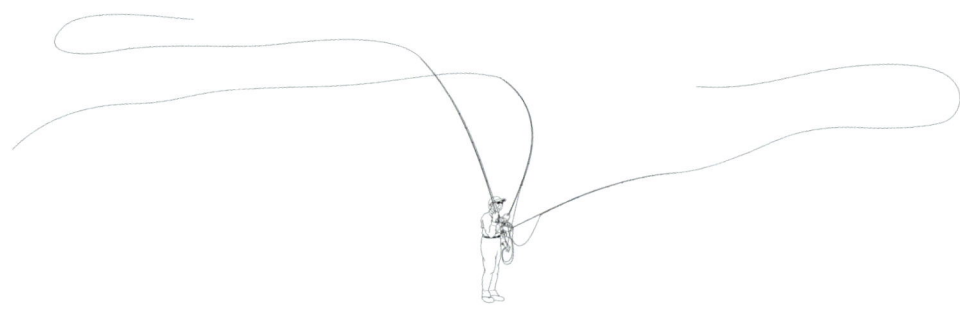

by a distinct pause, followed by the forward cast. This pause allows the fly line to unfurl or straighten out on the backcast, so that the rod can load properly before propelling the line forward on the forward cast.

Many beginning casters make the mistake of waving the rod like a metronome needle—back, forth, back, forth—but by doing this they fail to truly pause, and thus don't allow the rod to flex. I often tell these kinds of casters that the most important word they can learn is *Stop!* because without a definite stop, the backcast is compromised, and without a good backcast, the entire operation is compromised.

### What's the number one casting mistake and how do I solve it?

While guiding, I use many analogies to help beginning casters grasp this concept. I might say, for instance: *Pretend you are in a phone booth, and you are trying to hammer your way out of both sides of the booth.* Or perhaps: *Pretend you have stuck a potato on a fork, and you are trying to flick the potato at someone behind you, then, with the fork reloaded, flick a second potato at someone you're facing.*

You'll notice that both of these imaginary actions force the angler to concentrate on stopping, and more precisely, *an acceleration to a stop.* In the cast itself, the acceleration serves to generate line speed, which is essential to powering line, leader, and tippet through the inevitable wind.

### How do I tie better knots?

Of course, knots of many kinds link fly line to leader, leader to tippet, and tippet to fly, and many anglers fail to enter the fly-fishing arena because they fear having to learn dozens of new knots, etc. In truth, though, the angler can get by with only a few knots at his disposal: the nail knot, the triple surgeon's knot, the blood knot, and the clinch knot.

When tying the nail knot, it's best to use a tool (good ones can be purchased for about $10) until you become proficient; the triple surgeon's knot takes a bit longer than the double surgeon's but is infinitely stronger; and, when tied correctly, the clinch (note: not the improved

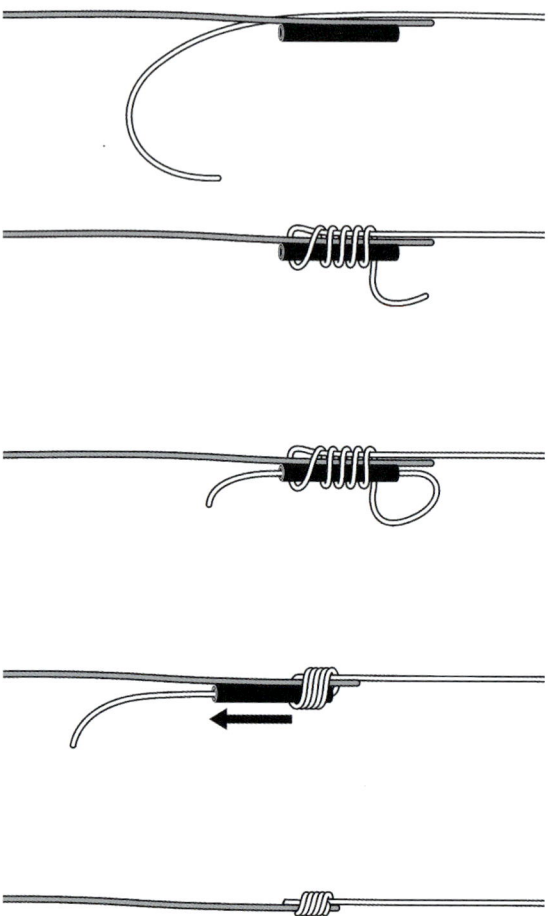

## Nail knot

This knot is used primarily to tie fly line to butt section, although it can be used in other applications when you need to tie a larger diameter line to a much smaller diameter line. There is rarely an on-stream application of this knot. Using a nail knot tool or a hollow tube, overlap the two lines. Holding the nail/tube and the lines together, wrap the lighter line around the nail/tube and both lines. Make six complete turns, pass the line through the loops (if using a nail) or through the tube (if using a tube or knot tool), and tighten the knot neatly around the nail or tube. Withdraw the nail or tube. Lubricate with saliva, pull the knot tight, and trim the ends.

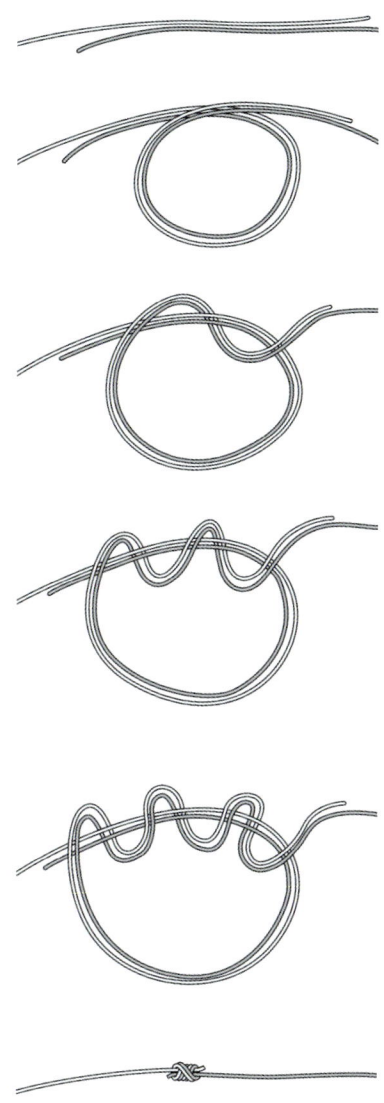

## Triple Surgeons Knot

A very easy knot to tie and effective for a number of applications, the triple surgeon's knot is best used for tying tippet to your leader or tippet to tippet. Place the leader and the tippet side by side. Use both lines to form a loop with enough overlap to tie a double overhand knot. Pull both ends through the loop and then through a second time. Lubricate the knot and pull it tight. Trim the ends.

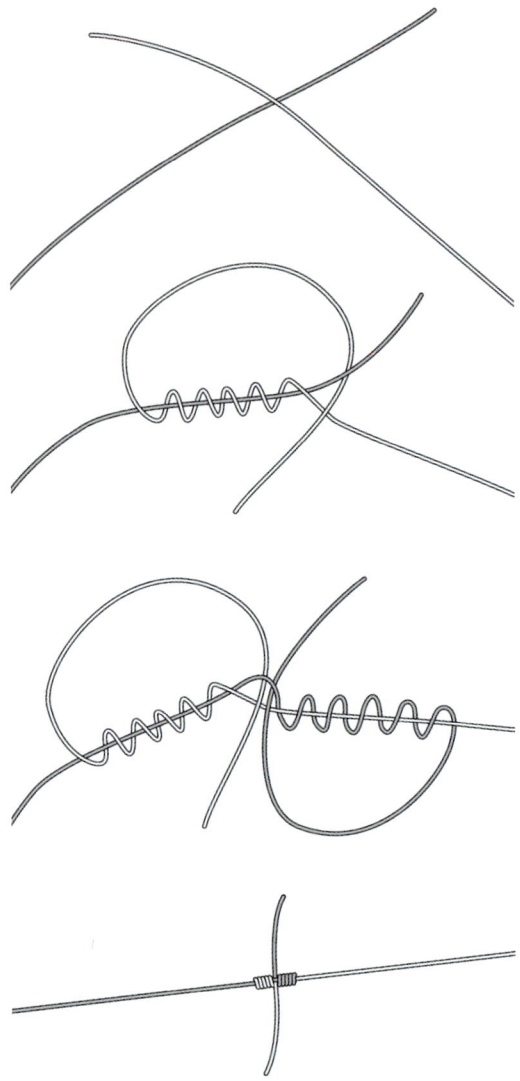

### Bloodknot

My favorite knot. A well-tied blood knot looks great on your leader, is sleek and sexy (yes, a knot can be sexy), and uses a lot less waste than a surgeons knot. Used for tying tippet to leader or tippet to tippet. Overlap the two lines to be joined. Wrap one end around the other line about six times. Tuck the end back between the lines. Repeat the process with the other line, tucking the end back between the lines in the opposite direction. Tighten and trim. Note: In nylon, tightening this knot alters the appearance.

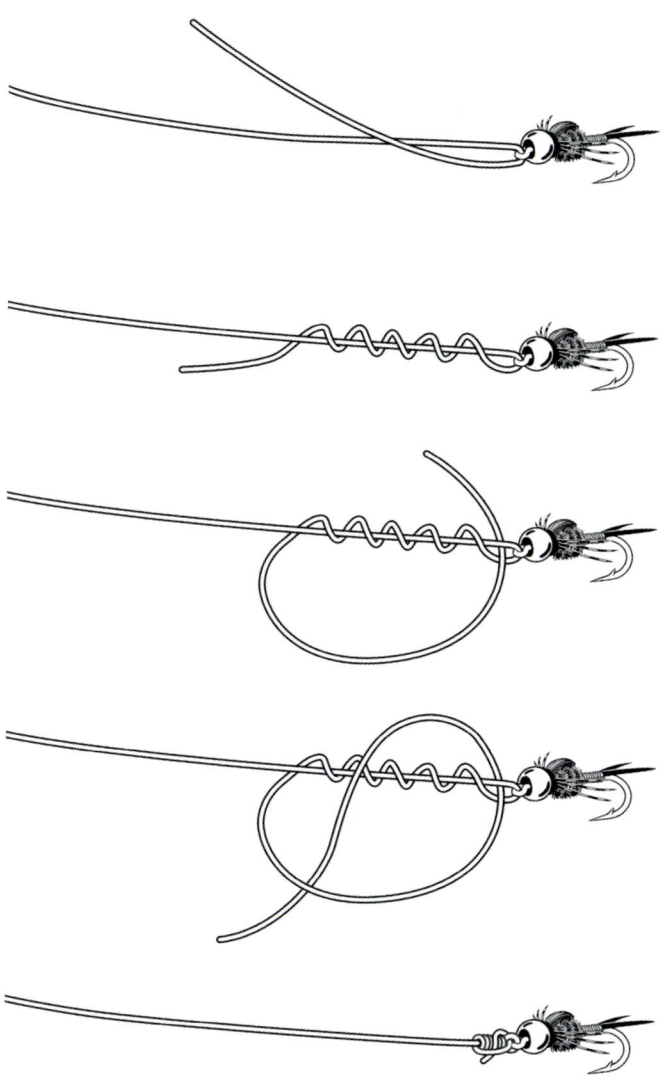

## Improved Clinch Knot

Used primarily for tying a fly to your tippet. Overlap the two lines to be joined.
Wrap one end around the other line about six times. Tuck the end back between
the lines. Repeat the process with the other line, tucking the end back between
the lines in the opposite direction. Tighten and trim. Note: In nylon, tightening
this knot alters the appearance.

clinch) is extremely tough. The key to tying these knots with proficiency is to practice at home until the process becomes part of habit.

When negotiating the knot becomes part of your muscle memory, you can trust yourself to tie it under pressure—say, when a dozen big bonefish are cruising your way on the flat, or when your hands are shaking in the falling snow and a 12-pound steelhead fins nearby.

## What piece of my gear should I improve immediately?

Sustained winds. Cold and wet weather. Unrelenting tropical sun. Saltwater. Big fish. These are the kinds of conditions that put your wits and gear to the test. Clients often ask me: What piece of gear should I improve on before all others? A good rod is essential, and a good line on a serviceable reel is important as well, but my answer may be surprising: get a better pair of waders. If you get an excellent, top-of-the-line pair of Gore-Tex breathable waders, you'll be more comfortable wherever and whenever you fish, no matter the conditions (some of the absolute best trout fishing occurs in the gnarliest months, such as late October and early March); if you're more

comfortable in all conditions, you'll go fishing more often; if you go fishing more often, you'll get better quicker; and the better you get, the more you'll enjoy yourself.

### How do I get a good drift with a dry fly?

A good pair of waders also allows the angler to wade boldly, and to better position himself or herself for a good cast and drift. Much of what helps us attain a good drift with a dry fly, or a nymph for that matter, isn't the distance or even the accuracy of the cast, but rather, its angle in relation to the river's currents. Time and time again while wade-guiding on the waters in Yellowstone National Park, I've watched very competent casters (but lazy waders) put themselves in poor position (with too many conflicting currents between themselves and the fly) and thus achieve dragging drifts. The angler willing to wade a bit farther will nearly always put herself in less-frequently-fished water, in better position to cast, manage line, and set the hook.

### Do I really need a strike indicator?

"Set!" the oft-frustrated guide yells throughout the day to his client. Usually, when fishing a reasonably sized dry fly, the angler can see her own fly get engulfed by the trout. Nymphing, however, presents a different kind of challenge since it requires knowing what's going on beneath the surface of the water. Most anglers employ a strike indicator, aka a float or a bobber, to help with this difficult task. The indicator's job is twofold: to suspend the flies above the bottom, and to "indicate" when the fly has been taken by a fish (or snagged debris). Indicators are made of cork, foam, plastic—heck, some guides even use balloons—and, yes, they are ugly and cumbersome to cast. Sometimes, as when tight-line nymphing or sight-nymphing in shallow water, an indicator isn't needed, but in general, the client's question, "Do I really need a strike indicator?" is met with this answer from the guide: "Only if you want to catch fish."

### How can I see more fish?

Simply put, indicators are tools that help us better envision what is taking place underwater. Another tool to help us see, literally, underwater, are polarized sunglasses, and they are as essential as a good pair of waders to increasing one's enjoyment astream. Polarized lenses cut the glare of the water's surface and allow anglers to locate fish and structure underwater. But seeing more fish while on the water is not just a matter of seeing below the surface; one must also learn to look for fish where they live: in front of or behind boulders, on color changes, near deadfalls and undercuts, etc.

### What do I do when I hook a big fish?

After years on the water, the experienced angler can begin to distill a river into its vital, fish-holding parts, and to "fish where the fish are." This awakening doesn't happen overnight, but rather after hours upon hours of dedicated observation. And when it does, the angler can expect to hook big fish more frequently. Now, how to handle these big fish—that's another story. My typical advice: "Let him run!!"

# Expert Advice: Matt Potter

## Breaking Habits:
## New Twists on Old Methods

*The Kingfisher*
Missoula, Montana
www.kingfisherflyshop.com

Born in Connecticut in 1967, Matt Potter caught his first trout, a brookie, on
Singleshanty Creek in the Adirondacks
on a sparsely tied Picket Pin. After honing his fly-fishing skills on the picky
trout of the Housatonic and Farming-
ton Rivers, Potter came west in 1986
to study zoology at the University of
Montana. His first guiding jobs came in
Alaska and the Soviet Far East, where

he developed innovative techniques, such as dead-drifting smolt patterns, for both anadromous and river-dwelling species. Returning to
Missoula to guide and run the outfitting for a local fly shop, Potter
quickly earned a reputation as the hardest working guide around on
Rock Creek and the Bitterroot, Blackfoot, and Clark Fork Rivers. In
1996, he and lifetime Missoula resident Jim Cox opened the Kingfisher Fly Shop, whose "fishing, not fashion" philosophy has made the
shop a favorite among local anglers—the Kingfisher has been voted
"Best of Missoula" in the *Independent* for seven years running. A
sixteen-year guiding veteran, Potter says his greatest accomplishment
as a guide is "the fact that clients who fished with me fifteen years ago
still want to fish with me as their guide. For me, it's always about having a good time. If panning for gold is your idea of a good time—and I

once had a client in Alaska who wanted to pan for gold all day—then we'll pan for gold." An accomplished fly tier and designer, Potter has created patterns that can be found in Umpqua Feather Merchants and Montana Fly Company catalogs. He also instructs the University of Montana's fly-fishing class.

*Like many Montana guides, you grew up in the East, fishing highly pressured, technical streams. What were the first differences you noticed between the rivers of your youth and the storied rivers of the West? And what tactical adjustments did you make when you began fishing big freestone rivers such as the Blackfoot and Clark Fork?*

Well, the people are nicer out here! Seriously, I think people require more space in the West. In the East, folks don't mind fishing 10 yards from the next angler, and that creates conflicts, but out here there's just a lot more space afforded the next guy—on most rivers. You have to stake out your spot in the East, sit on a hole all evening, or risk not finding a good run to fish. Out here, in my manic fishing stage, I had much more of a "run-and-gun" take on fishing: I would give a run a dozen good drifts and move on to the next riffle. Nowadays, I'm going back in the other direction and enjoying catching a few tough fish from one spot, rather than having to rip all the lips in the river.

*As an experienced fisherman learning to guide less-experienced anglers, how did you change your tactics to accommodate the skills of clients?*

When I first started guiding, I found this very difficult. The ways you might catch fish don't always work for your clients. Guiding, simply put, is an extension of fishing. A good guide is really just fishing using an intermediary, as it were, and sometimes that intermediary is a handicap to the guide. The good guide is going to do whatever it takes technique-wise or fly-selection-wise to give their client the best chance to catch fish.

I remember a time up in Alaska, fishing on the Igulapek River, where the rainbows were taking mayfly nymphs very delicately, and I was mentally fixated on the idea that the big rainbows would only take a perfectly dead-drifted nymph. I was walking the boat down the river and finally noticed that both clients were missing numerous takes, but the guy in the back of the boat was hooking more fish because his flies were dragging just a bit—there was just a tad more tension on his line. So I started telling the guys to cast at a slight downstream angle; this way the current would put a gradual J-hook in the line, and my clients began hooking fish immediately. It's not necessarily the "right" way to do things, but it worked great for two guys who were having a hard time detecting subtle takes.

Eventually, I learned that it's no longer about how *you* would fish, but about adapting. For instance, some of the toughest fish in the Missoula area are Clark Fork fish in the fall. These big, shallow-water rainbows see a lot of artificial flies; they require long leaders and fine tippets, and I would prefer to fish them with a low-riding, nearly invisible dry fly. It was hard for a lot of anglers, so I began to approach these fish in a different way, by having guys swing small, un-weighted pheasant tail nymphs through the risers—a kind of Leisenring-lift type presentation. This worked well, except the light tippet on the swing would break almost immediately. Eventually, I discovered those Rio shock-absorber leaders, with the foot-long piece of rubber toward the top of the leader, and our ratio of strikes to fish landed skyrocketed.

*Most people think in terms of dead-drifting nymphs, stripping streamers, and floating dry flies without much action. As an innovative guide, how do you alter these techniques to specific situations and client levels?*

I remember my first or second year of guiding, during a tough week of post-runoff fishing, when Jim Cox came into the fly shop one day and told me that he had hammered the Clark Fork fish by dead-drifting Wooly Buggers with a San Juan worm for a trailer. I looked him straight in the eye and said, "What?! You trailed a streamer with a San Juan worm?" Sure enough, he did, and the technique has become quite standard on our rivers by now.

A few years later we modified the technique to fish the Missouri when the river was running near 20,000 cubic feet per second. Even the locals said the river was blown out! To imitate the crayfish in the shallows, we started fishing brown, lead-eye crystal buggers tight— tight!—to the banks. The trick, though, was that we had clients dead-drift this rig on a clear slime-line with just 3–4 feet of leader so that the connection to the fly would be extremely direct. Now, we didn't catch fish everywhere, but in certain places—behind islands, on slow, inside seams—we really took it to them and made a day of it.

*What are some other out-of-the-box techniques that you've put into practice?*
Well, this isn't really a fishing technique, but when I used to guide on Rock Creek, the flows were traditionally in the 1200–1500 c.f.s. range, which means the river was moving at a pretty good clip. If a client would break his salmon fly off in the willows, he would have to go without a bug for a few good minutes—it would be two or three bends before I could find slow enough water to anchor in. So at the beginning of each day I would de-barb and gink up about a dozen salmon fly patterns, and put them in a Styrofoam cup that the client would keep in the cup holder of the boat. This way, provided he could tie a simple clinch knot, he wouldn't have to wait so long to fish again.

And speaking of the Creek, there were a few years when fishing a small, black glow bug to imitate egg clusters worked well as a salmon fly trailer.

*Do you find these kinds of tricks only work on freestone rivers, where the fish are generally a bit less selective?*
No, I think people often give spring creek fish more credit than they're due. My favorite pattern for most spring creeks and sloughs is a small, un-weighted damselfly nymph. Anytime a fish is cruising just beneath the surface, not feeding in a consistent rhythm, this is the bug I go to. It also works on rising fish if you cast it a few feet out in front of the

riser and give it a little twitch. I've seen this work on local waters, but also the famous spring creeks like Armstrong's and DePuy's. And a big chunk of protein like a wooly bugger on a creek like that is deadly. People just don't try it often enough.

*Jim Cox sounds like one of the people you've learned a good deal from in this business.*

Jim is one of the most innovative people I've ever fished with. He's a relentless experimenter, and he won't count any fly out until he's tried it. He was the first guy I ever saw who tied on a huge red, like a #6, Turk's Tarantula and rolled it through the deep holes on the Blackfoot in the middle of an August day. Most guys were nymphing that late on a 100-degree day, but Jim started catching big cutthroat with regularity this way, and I became a believer.

His favorite bug on the lower Clark Fork in the late evening was and still is a Badger Potts fly, a woven-body horsehair fly from the 1950s. He would take this fly and swing it through swirlies and back-eddies that the lower Clark is famous for, and the tough caddis-sippers would tear it apart. And you know, late in the day, without the eyes of a guide, that was the only way his clients were going to catch those fish.

A few years later, I remembered that technique when those very realistic epoxy minnows came out; I would have clients swing them through the pickiest trico-sippers, and that fly fished that particular way worked wonders.

*You and Jim have been productive and innovative fly designers for the past few years. As a guide and tier, what exactly are you looking for in a fly these days?*

Basically Jim and I look at it this way: anything that can be done has essentially been done. The guy who invented the parachute Adams, or the guy who invented the Chernobyl Ant, now those guys were innovative. These days, though, it's just variations on a theme. We're looking for triggering, lifelike motion—some aspect of the fly that's going to make a fish move out from under that log, or up from the bottom, and help compensate for the client's normal inability to get the fly close to the cover.

*Your shop, the Kingfisher, has one of the largest, if not largest, fly selections in Montana. What are some of the biggest mistakes you see anglers make when buying flies?*

Here in Missoula, I see a lot of people buying flies that are too small. They think a fly has to be small to work because they're used to seeing only caddis and mayflies in the air. I also notice people who get fixated on certain things, like the name of the fly. For instance, just because a Goddard caddis doesn't say "capnia stonefly" on it doesn't mean it isn't one of the best early-season stonefly imitations around. There are also a ton of "triggers" out there in the fly bins, and not all of these "triggers" work as well on fish as they do on the buyer.

*What changes or innovations do you see the next ten years bringing to the fly-tying world?*

Well, I think of it this way: Ten years ago, much of the fly-tying material that we carry didn't exist. The shop might have carried rubber legs, but just in black and white, whereas today we have an infinite number of sizes and shades. I don't know for sure. Maybe there will be some sort of movement back to natural materials. But I think people will continue to go to craft stores and keep using the synthetics. I bet 10 to 20 percent of the flies we carry don't have a single natural fiber on them—that's wild. And I'll bet that 90 percent of the flies we carry have at least one synthetic piece of material in their recipe.

As far as innovation goes, I think fish get very pattern specific. About ten years ago, Pat Berry's Wing-Thing was a very popular fly around here. It was tied to float low, in the surface film, and its profile fooled a lot of fish. But after about three or four years, the fish seemed to get wise to something about it. Now it's coming around again. But I think if you don't tweak your patterns a little bit each year, you're not doing enough experimentation to make a big discovery.

*As an instructor in the University of Montana's fly-fishing class, you teach your students a great deal about reading water. How do you help them break down a big Western river into manageable chunks?*

When we discuss reading water, we begin by walking down to the Clark Fork and taking a look at it. We divide the water into traditional sections—riffles, runs, pools—and talk about typical flies and techniques for these spots. We generalize about trout needs, where the fish might be and why they might be there, and then show them various slides and diagrams. I try to remind them at some point that the only fish you can catch are the fish you can reach, so start close and don't try to cover the entire river all at once.

*Are there any instances where you see these traditional holding spots varying from river to river, season to season?*

The Bitterroot is a place this happens often. Trout have certain spots they prefer to hold, prime lies, say, behind a log, next to an undercut bank and a good foam line. But on a river like the Bitterroot where this fish might get run over by seventeen boats a day, the fish will move to a different lie so that they're not being harassed all the time by boats and flies. We find in the Bitterroot that some of the biggest fish are found in shallow insides where most folks don't think to fish.

A lot of this information is stuff I've arrived at after failing with normal techniques; you sort of reach a level of frustration and begin experimenting. I've located a lot of summertime spring holes on the Clark Fork by skin-diving, just feeling the change of temperature on my body. And I've lucked into great sloughs on the Bitterroot by literally killing time while guiding. This is stuff that really can't be taught, but has to be learned by spending countless hours on the water.

*There's certainly been an increase in the number of guides in Montana in the past ten years. What changes can we anticipate in the next decade in the fishing, guiding, and outfitting worlds of Montana?*

I think that people will have to continually evolve their techniques and patterns. When I first started guiding, a #14 parachute Adams would get me through the season. But fish these days require more intricate patterns and, for the most part, better presentations. They're more easily spooked and less tolerant of mess-ups. We know for sure that the resource is healthier now than it's been in the last fifty years, so as long as we continue to take care of habitat, the fish will be there, just tougher to catch.

I also see a lot of good things happening on the conservation front. Here in Missoula, the Milltown Dam removal has been a long time coming. It's amazing to me that our country has gone from building dams a few decades ago to attempting to remove them now. I think it shows that economically, if we do the math, we have much more to gain from clean, undammed water and its benefits than we do from keeping dams around. Sure, there will be some sort of short-term sacrifice financially for outfitters here in Missoula (with the removal of the dam), but the long-term benefits far outweigh the difficulties.

**Quick-Glance Summary:**

Experiment, modify, change

Think outside the fly box

Tweak your patterns

Something old can be new again

Minnows during a mayfly hatch

Dropper nymph on a streamer

Triggers

Start close

# Up in the Air

### Improving Your Cast.
### Longer, Easier, and More Efficient

## Do my hands work together?

One of the first questions an angler should ask oneself when attempting to improve on casting distance is: Are my right and left hands working in concert with one another? We call these two hands "the line hand and the rod hand," and their chief roles are self-evident: one hand controls the rod while the other controls the line. Right-handed casters hold the rod in their right hand and the line in their left; left-handed casters, of course, do the opposite. The line hand's tug on the line at the beginning of each cast is called a "haul," and nearly every proficient caster practices "the double-haul," which is a cast that employs two hauls: one as the backcast begins, and one as the forward cast begins.

## What is a double-haul?

Using the double-haul is almost essential to becoming a better fly fisher. Similar to learning to drive a stick shift—you either can or you can't, but you have to invest time in learning. Joan Wulff best sums up the double-haul with this quote:

"It makes casting long line easier, so that you can fish all day and not tire. What happens is that by using that second hand you are adding speed to your line. The rod is loaded more deeply, and that transfers to greater energy in your line. And you need high line speed for longer casts, or for casting into wind."

Begin with your backcast as normal. The moment you begin to apply power on your backcast, give a slight tug on the fly line you're holding in your line hand. We call this tug a "haul." Do not let go of the fly line. Allow your line hand to move backward with your rod hand as your backcast lays out behind you. You can say to yourself "up" as you start your backcast and haul immediately after you say "up." By saying this you are allowing yourself the necessary time for the application of power in your casting stroke to happen before you haul.

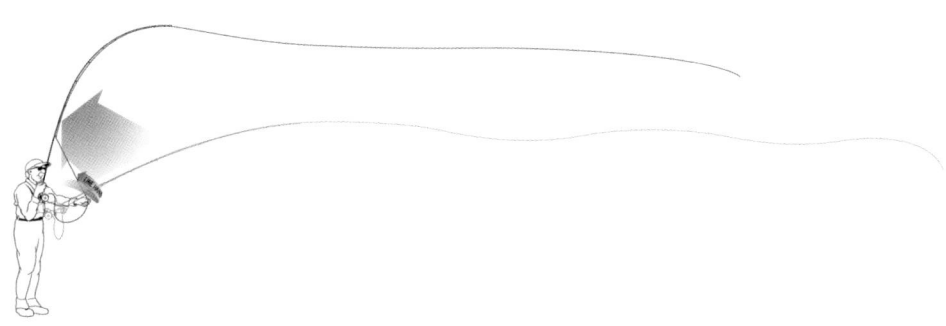

This stage happens as you are coming forward out of your backcast into your forward cast or your presentation cast. As you are applying power in your forward cast, give another haul with your line hand. Say "down" when you begin applying power and then haul immediately after you say "down." The "up" and "down" terms come from Mel Krieger, one of the best of casting instructors.

Until the angler learns to "double-haul," he or she will be at the mercy of that four-letter elemental word: wind. If timed right, the hauls the angler makes with the line hand flex the rod thoroughly and help generate line speed, a key to accurate and distance casting. To grasp the concept of line speed, I ask you to think for a moment about baseball. It's a windy night in October, and the wind is blowing in hard from the outfield—who is most likely to be a successful hitter, the line-drive singles hitter, or the big-swinging home run king? The line-drive hitter is bound to have more success on a windy night because the balls he hits will be driven with more speed, closer to the ground, and thus less susceptible to the invisible wall of wind. Similarly, the angler who learns to double-haul crisply and with harnessed power will be more effective in the wind than the he-man who tries to muscle his cast out there.

### Why is my backcast so important?

As Norman Maclean wrote decades ago, "Until man is redeemed, he will always take the rod too far back on his backcast." Much has changed in the fishing world since Maclean wrote—we have blogs, online fly shops, chat rooms, hatch reports, etc., these days—but Maclean's statement still holds true. The backcast is much like a back swing in the world of golf: No matter how good your forward swing, you can't overcome a bad back swing. Taking the rod too far back on the backcast causes myriad problems: It throws the line into the water behind the angler instead of into the air, impeding the forward cast; it opens the casting loop, decreasing accuracy; and it just plain looks bad.

### Why did my line pile in front of me?

If you're wondering why your line lands in a pile out in front of you instead of shooting out like a laser, it's probably because you're taking your backcast too far back. In Maclean's days, when most anglers fished with slower bamboo rods, the adage "make the cast between ten and two" was adhered to, meaning that if high noon were indicated by the rod held straight up, directly overhead, then the backcast stopped at ten o'clock, and the forward cast stopped at two. These days, however, with the advent of faster graphite rods, the cast can more accurately be said to occur between eleven and one o'clock.

### How do I beat this wind?

Another reason the line might be landing in a pile at your feet is because the wind is blowing in your face. Wind is a relative term. The same expert who easily throws a 100-foot cast into a 40-mile Bahamian headwind at a tailing bonefish will have trouble punching a 15-foot leader tapered to 7x on a spring creek while tossing a 3-weight to rising cutthroat on DePuy's Spring Creek. To a beginning caster, a 5 mile-per-hour breeze might thwart the cast; whereas an experienced caster can put a fly on a pie plate at 75 feet despite a 30-mile-per-hour easterly blowing straight up Paradise Valley. The difference: line speed and size of casting loop. The more line speed one can generate (think: condense the casting motion, use more energy in a smaller space), the tighter one can keep the casting loop, and the tighter the loop, the more readily the line cuts through wind.

### What is a reach cast?

Line speed and tight casting loops also allow anglers to more easily make casts that are essential to good fly presentation, such as the roll cast (for use in tight situations), side-arm cast (which helps cut through wind), and the all-important reach cast. Because it allows the angler to place the fly downstream from the fly line and ensures the fly itself floats drag free, the reach cast is the most important arrow in the trout angler's quiver. A standard cast coupled with an upstream mend will fool trout fairly consistently, but the reach cast

Consider this cast as an "in-the-air mend." It is ideal for fishing from a boat or presenting a fly to spooky fish. As your fly line straightens out in front of you (as the forward casting loop is opening up), slowly pull the rod through the air toward the direction you wish to mend. This will change the position of the straightened fly line before it lands.

(often called a reach mend) is needed if the angler wishes to regularly fool large selective trout, especially on spring creeks and great hatch rivers such as the Bitterroot, where long downstream drifts with light tippets are paramount.

## What is an S cast?

Fancier casts, such as the curve cast, which help the angler hook the fly under branches or overhanging grasses, are fun to learn and employ, but aren't incredibly useful on a day-to-day basis. The S cast—a cast made downstream, and one in which the angler finishes by wiggling some slack into the line—can be of help when conflicting river currents make drag-free drifts difficult.

Ideal for adding slack to your drift *before* your fly line lands on the water. Moments before you present the fly and line onto the water, gently squiggle some slack into the straightened fly line. This is best accomplished by feeding line with your line hand and shaking your rod hand as if you were trying to scrape ice off a windshield—small jerks and shakes.

## What about casting in tight quarters?

As a kid plying the small waters near Bozeman, I was always intrigued by the bow-and-arrow cast, where the angler pulls the fly toward himself (thus bending the rod into a bow shape) then lets it spring out over the water. After poking myself pretty badly a few times, I realized that the roll cast was a more effective, if safer, option for casting in tight quarters.

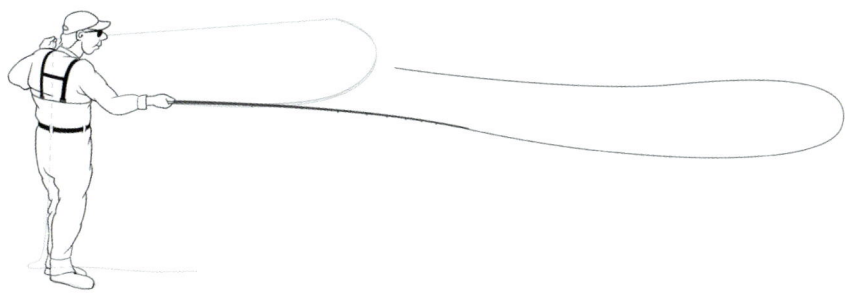

This cast is *the* cast to use in extremely tight quarters with brush overhead. Begin by having some slack line out of your rod tip. This slack line will eventually "shoot" out of your rod tip after you release the loaded rod. The cast begins by pulling back on the fly until you get a bend in the rod through the midsection. When ready, let go of the fly. There is little need for a tenkara rod when you can master the bow-and-arrow cast.

## I want to cast 100 feet. Do I need to?

Another task I became obsessed with as a young angler was casting 100 feet of fly line. Taller and bigger than me, my brother Carl was a born distance-caster and I could never quite stretch my casts as far as he could. Whether we were fishing the lower Madison in Beartrap Canyon or some high country lake, his fly would always land a leader's length farther out than mine. So I learned to study the water closer to where I stood and quickly found that there was always prudent water to ply within 50 feet or less of where I waded. As a freshwater guide, it's always nice to have a "hucker" in the boat, someone who can really "air it out," but the folks who catch the most fish cast 50 to 60 feet with accuracy and manage their line diligently. Whether guiding or fishing on my own, I'll take an absolutely precise 40-foot cast over an "in-the-ballpark" 100-foot cast any day.

# Expert Advice: Paul Roos

## Casting: The Basics to Special Casts and Techniques

*Paul Roos Outfitters* and *The Oxbow Land Company*
Ovando, Montana

Born and raised in the headwaters of the Blackfoot River near Lincoln, Montana, Paul Roos grew up exploring and fishing the Blackfoot and its smaller forks. Blanketed by lush lodgepole and ponderosa pines, the headwaters of the Blackfoot remain a special place for Paul and the anglers who visit the area. As a kid, he learned fly fishing through  trial and error as he spent the bulk of his days trouncing around the area waters. After high school in Augusta and four years of college, Paul settled in Helena, Montana. For nearly twenty years Paul taught high school math, and he quickly learned that teaching came easy for him. In the summers between school years, Paul learned the unique traits good guides required by Pat Barnes, Montana's first licensed outfitter. After working under Pat, Paul hung out his own shingle and created Paul Roos Outfitters (PRO). Today, PRO is one of the more respected fishing outfitters in the state. Paul no longer runs the business, but that is just fine with him—it allows him to guide more and have "more a presence on the front lines" where he can teach and guide on a daily basis. Paul has an electric smile and a contagious laugh, which surely helps his students and clients increase their learning curve. In addition to guiding full time, Paul has created the Oxbow Land Company, a small collection of landowners, businesses, and conservationists committed to preserving large tracts of land, the ranching lifestyle, all while remaining committed to conservation and restoration.

*Were you formally taught how to cast?*

Not really. Growing up, I would fish a lot with my dad. During that time of the century, and especially in the West, there was a lot to be said for learning things on your own—you know, the trial-and-error of it all. Plus, I think my dad really enjoyed fishing and wanted to fish and knew I would figure it out.

*So you would say you were self-taught?*

Yes and no. I had a lot of friends and we fished together a lot, and my dad would help every so often, but for the most part, it was just me, the rod, and the stream, and I would have to figure it all out myself. My father was a wonderful instructor, but there was still much of the older Montana mind-set of "just get it done."

*What about your first fish?*

I don't remember my very first fish, but I remember the one I caught all by myself. My dad tied on a Grey Echo Yellow, where we were fishing on a small creek near Lincoln. My dad had gone around the bend, and I hooked, caught, and landed a fish all alone. I don't remember the actual fish and what it looked like, but I remember the whole experience of being out.

*What was the biggest hurdle or problem when you were learning to cast—can you remember?*

That's easy. It was learning to be patient. As a kid and a beginner, it was hard to develop skill while being focused on fishing. I did a lot of things wrong—like trying to cast faster or more aggressive. Patience and casting with a slower rhythm were key. Looking back, perhaps fishing taught me patience, or, perhaps teaching sixth and seventh graders taught me patience!

*Now that we've talked a little about your past and how you learned how to cast, imagine I am a first-timer, a never-ever. There is a "fly pole" sitting on the ground, and by the end of the day I want to catch fish.*

First, I would spend a lot of time to truly get anglers to get a sense of what is success. In other words, redefining success. It is not about catching fish. For the first few minutes I will just talk about what fly fishing has brought me—great friends, some hilarious times, some enriching times. I would stress that I don't always remember how many fish or how big of fish that were caught. Then I would explain the basic concept and perhaps cast a little while talking.

*When might you introduce the equipment?*

Right now I would let them get a feel for it, grasp it all, play around with it some. Let them see that it is fragile and an important tool, but at the same time they need not be overly anxious or timid.

*Once they understand how to hold the rod, what's next?*

I have them hold the line in their line hand. Left hand for right-handed casters and right hand for left-handed casters. Remember, this is all a process and some people will learn quicker than others and it will be very tough for some. From my teaching days I know that some people don't learn until they are ready to learn. In fly fishing you have to stress that you are using the rod to move the fly line. A key point in that is the fly line must be straight before it will move. A good analogy is a sprinkler spraying a yard. Imagine you're in that yard and want to water a different patch of grass so you must move the sprinkler, but you do not want to get wet or turn off the water. In order to do so you must pull the hose until all the coils are out and then the sprinkler will move. This is a good analogy and works with most anglers. The same is true for your basic casting stroke—get the line straight then accelerate the line.

*That makes sense with the line, but what do you want the rod to do?*

The rod needs to be accelerated through the air as well, but it also must be loaded, or forced into a bend. I do this by grasping the end of about 30 feet of straightened-out fly line out from their rod tip. I grasp the line in my hands. I tell them to point the rod toward me and grab the rod with their rod hand, as if they were shaking hands with the rod. I tell them to move the rod slowly and with even force or effort to about the ten o'clock position.

*Wait a second? Explain ten o'clock?*

A lot of instructions use a clock face as a reference to teach casting. It is also a good tool to use when learning to cast. Imagine you hold your arms directly over your head, as if signaling a three-point bucket in a basketball game. Your hands are at the NOON position when they are pointing directly ahead of you. From there, focus only on one hand. Straight up is NOON and straight down, through your body, as if you were to draw a line pointing down your Achilles' heel, is six o'clock. Toward the direction you are casting is three o'clock and three o'clock being parallel to the ground. Nine o'clock is parallel to the ground behind the direction you are casting.

*So, once they are slowly moving the rod back and then get to the ten o'clock position, what next?*

I then tell them to accelerate the rod quickly back, but stop it and their hand which is holding the rod, stop it right when their hand and rod-hand are at their ear. The ear, which would be, ideally at the twelve o'clock position. I do that once—just once. I then ask some questions. "Where is the rod pointing? Did the rod bend? What about the fly line?"

*Why these questions?*

The fly line will follow the rod tip, so you want them to begin to think about some of the physics. And people learn in different ways—some by doing, some by picturing it in their head, most by a combination. Asking questions just makes them think.

*Okay, so now the rod is back in the twelve o'clock or one o'clock position behind their head, stopped. What next?*

I walk behind them and pick up the fly line off the ground. I straighten it out by walking back a little more. I hold the line. If you are learning on your own, find someone to help with this. Next I tell the angler to move the rod forward to the ten o'clock position, putting a bend in the rod. We call this "loading the rod" or forcing a bend in the rod.

*Is this crucial to a good cast?*

Yes. Many instructors say "let the rod do the work"; well, unless beginners can actually feel the bend, it is hard for them to grasp that principle. The rod is a tool, and all beginners need to know that and then see and feel how it works.

*So you have the caster standing, rod bending, you holding the line. What next?*

I tell them to move the rod forward with the bend in it while I am holding the line. Then they must move the rod forward to ten o'clock and make a quick stop. They must accelerate and then STOP! I would do this line grab a dozen or so times so they get the idea of the quick stop. The line should cast out straight in front of them. This will come in handy later when we cover shooting line.

*What would you say are some of the most important things in this first step?*

Energizing the line and stopping sharply. By energizing the line, I mean using the rod as tool. Plus it is also now essential to separate the casts into a backcast and forward cast.

*How do you get anglers to separate between the two?*

Make them work on a pick-up and lay-down cast. They start with about 30 feet of fly line on the ground in front of them. They pick up or raise the rod to get the slack out. I remind them of me grabbing the line making it straight, as the same principle applies here. If you have too much or too little slack, the rod will not have enough time to accelerate to make the line straight. The analogy of the sprinkler works for this as well.

*Do anglers struggle with the pick-up and lay-down cast?*

Some do, some don't. The pick-up is to get the slack out of the line. The lay-down is after you've loaded the rod and the line casts straight out in front. It is just another way to call it when you combine all the parts of the whole.

*And what would you call the parts of the whole?*

"Pick-up" is picking up or taking out the slack. Next is the "backcast," where you accelerate the rod in a straight line back. The "forward cast" is what you did when the line was held behind you and you forced the rod into a bend. And the lay-down is simply lowering the rod AFTER you have made a quick stop when you've come forward.

*What do find yourself telling anglers during all of this?*

You just have to keep focused on acceleration and a quick stop. On the pick-up and lay-down, when starting your backcast, get the rod tip up during your pick-up, point it to the sky or ceiling, and then move it in a straight line over your head and make a quick stop.

*Are they done yet?*

No. Not at all! Now we've got to add the other hand, or the "line hand." This hand is used in casting to change the length of the line during cast. They grab the rod with their casting arm and then grab the fly line with their line hand. They pinch the line between their thumb and index finger. At this point I add another term into the game. "Strip."

### How do you teach this as anglers strip line for so many reasons?
Easy. I walk out with a large length of line and then have them strip it back. It is very important they make little strips—like 6 inches each time. This will help in later uses. And to let the line pile at their feet. Once they've stripped in enough line, usually you need about 20 feet of line out, or when learning laying on the ground, before you can go into your pick-up and lay-down cast.

### When do you strip in line?
You must strip in line if there is too much line out to get out all the slack. Knowing this will just come with more practice and time.

### You've got the angler stripping in line, they have done a pick-up and lay-down cast, now you've got to get them casting longer and shooting line. What's next?
They should strip in about 8 feet of fly line and have it at their feet. I remind them of me holding the line behind them and the acceleration stop that must happen to get the line to cast out straight in front of them. Then they just practice that, BUT at the moment the fly line passes over the rod tip, and they might have to watch the fly line, I tell them to let go of the line in their line hand. It will take a few tries, but eventually they will shoot out that 8 feet of fly line. Just do this several times and you should see some success. They should see and hear the line make a small slapping sound as it shoots through the guides and even slaps the rod a little as it gets tight against the rod.

### When do you add the false casting so they can get a long cast?
I don't really call it false casting, but more like making second and third casts, as I try to get anglers to not false cast as the fish are in the water not the air. But I tell them to master shooting line first, then

gradually work on adding line WHILE casting. The principles are the same, except instead of entirely letting go of the line on the forward cast, they should let loose or un-pinch a small amount. This actually comes easier than you would think—most folks figure out when to add the line. Where they get caught is not accelerating and stopping quick enough or soon enough in the cast.

*What about their "casting loop"?*

I usually wait a few lessons or some time before I cover this. But I show them what is meant by a casting loop. In summary a casting loop is when the fly line passes over your head after you've stopped the rod on the backcast or forward cast. It is created when you accelerate and stop. If you watch the fly line as it passes over your head, it will make an elongated U or there will be a top and a bottom, the bottom being the line that is coming closest to the rod tip. This U, which will flatten out after you stop and PAUSE, is called the casting loop. I guess "casting loop" sounded better than "casting U"!

*Whoa, wait a second here, this is first time you mentioned a pause in a cast, Explain?*

Just like the sprinkler analogy—the line must be straight before you can move it where you want it to go—the fly line has to be straight. So, after accelerating and stopping on either back or forward casts, you must wait for the loop to straighten out. Once the loop, or U, is straight then you can make your next forward or backcast. This principle was shown when I stood behind a caster and held the line as they moved the rod forward, bending the rod. If there is no pause, rod cannot be loaded.

*What about all this talk about casting tight loops?*

A tight loop is a loop where the top of the U is closer to the bottom of the U. This is achieved by accelerating and stopping the rod in a much faster or quicker time frame or the distance that the rod tip travels in the air is closer together. Tight loops are often desired, but there are times when you want a wide loop. My guess is that you will cover those later in the book.

*How might an angler practice casting a tighter loop?*
Focus on shortening the distance the rod tip travels in the air and working on adding line to your cast by a longer acceleration and a quicker stop. But, remember the more line you have out and the longer your cast, the longer it will take the line to straighten on your forward and backcasts. So, you must pause and wait after you accelerate and stop so the line can be straight behind or in front of you. If the line is not straight when you start a back or forward cast, you will not have tight loop and may not even have a cast at all!

*How do anglers improve on all of these techniques?*
Practice, practice, practice. Both on the ground and on the water. We've just only covered getting the line out there, so before you can really fish, you must be able to cast. Hunters don't spend time and effort to get a critter if they don't spend lots of time learning to shoot.

*What are some other more specialized casts that you might teach if someone is really moving along fast?*
A roll cast is an important one to have in your arsenal. It is just a modified forward cast. You move the rod tip back, without actually casting, to where you would normally stop it on a backcast. Then you accelerate quickly and stop quickly where you would stop on a normal forward cast. You must have sufficient line out and the slack out of the line before you go slide the line back to where you begin the roll cast. A roll cast works well when you've got trees or rocks behind you and you cannot make a backcast.

## *What about the "roll cast and pick up"?*

Another good cast to learn early on. You roll-cast line out and then right when the line hits the water and is straight in front of you, immediately go into your acceleration on your backcast. Just like in the pick-up and lay-down, but you're adding a roll cast before the pick-up. This cast is a great way to get more fishing in and less casting.

## *So, do you separate between the two?*

Yes—you bet. Fishing is when your fly is on the water. Casting is when you are changing the location of your fly. You really aren't fishing unless your fly is in a spot where a fish can eat it. And that is usually not in the air or tangled in the bushes! (Roos lets out a big laugh.) And we've all been in the bushes a lot.

## *After all we've talked about, would you say that most anglers would be ready to go fishing?*

Yes. With enough practice and some patience during the fishing as everyone has a learning curve. Fly fishing is a process, and if you hit the water too early, you may get frustrated. Just take a little time to learn. Take the time to master the pick-up and lay-down cast, shooting line, and getting the line hand to work together with your rod hand.

## *How might you describe an intermediate caster?*

I would classify them in five ways. First, they know how to cast line out. They can cast 30 or so feet of line out in a straight line in front of them. Second, they truly know when to stop the rod at the right time and know how to cast a tight loop and a large loop. Third, they have an idea of presenting the fly, but may not always get it just right. But they catch fish sometimes because the fish doesn't know they are an intermediate caster! Fourth, they are just beginning to understand how the position of their body can help or hinder their casts—kneeling, casting over their opposite shoulder, dealing with wind, etc. Lastly, they have a rough idea of line management and the various mends or motions needed to have more success. I might also throw in that they begin to grasp the idea of stealth in fishing—the idea that they are hunting fish and seek out those opportunities.

*For these intermediate and experienced casters, what might be some special casts that you use to keep your fly in the water more than in the air?*

I like a 'shotgun' or 'target' cast. Aim at a point that is actually under the water near where you want the fly to land. Really drive the rod tip and stop it fast. This works well in fast water. When the fly line lands you will have some excess slack and you will need to strip like hell to get the slack out so you can set the hook. I also use a 'parachute cast' often. If there is lots of wind or I am fishing from the back I use this cast. I overcast the amount of line and leader I need and allow it to pile up above the fish or zone I am fishing. Lastly I use a 'roll-roll' cast if I am fishing water behind a rock that lies in fast water. I set up the drift I want by painting a picture in my brain of where I want the fly. Then it starts with a roll cast then another roll cast right after that so I am piling up the leader and fly line in the faster water while the fly sits in the slower water. That way the excess fly line and leader won't drag the fly out.

*What is the next level of caster after intermediate, and how do anglers know they might be there?*

I would say it is one where you become more of a hunter. You seek out specific fish or look for the tough spots or challenging fish. Perhaps you want to fish just certain types of waters—small streams, spring creeks, tailwaters, only float fish, etc. It really is about what you want from the sport. That's the beauty of fly fishing—there is something in it for everyone.

*Any last thoughts?*

I think along with progressing through the beginner to expert stage of fly fishing, most, if not all, anglers who consider themselves fly fishers should also have a conservation ethic. Just as we presently enjoy fly fishing, we need to make sure the resources are around so our younger generations can enjoy what we have now.

## Quick-Glance Summary:

Learning to cast takes time—trial and error

Be patient, while learning and in your stroke

Get the slack out then accelerate

If you can feel the rod bend, then you are loading it

Accelerate and STOP!

With your line hand strip little strips

Learn to shoot line first, then work to add line in your casts

Wait for your casting loop to straighten

Practice, practice, practice

# Chapter Three

# Humans Are from Land; Fish Are from Water

## Unlocking Your Inner Fish-Finder

### What do fish need?

Oxygen, shelter, food; cool water, cover, grub; in other words, some-thing to breathe, somewhere to hide, something to eat: these above all trout require for survival. Riffles and rapids are more oxygenated than slow-moving pools, so trout tend to seek out the bumpy water when air temperature is hot; but the faster-moving water also requires more energy to hold in, so trout tend to seek out deep pools and glides in spring and late fall when air and water temperature have dropped.

Because a trout's lie often depends heavily on its current food source, we can simplify a trout's holding spots into two categories: holding lies and feeding lies. With the advent of radio-telemetry tracking, the age-old idea of the grandad trout that sits under a log for its whole life was put to bed. We know now that trout move great distances with great regularity, usually in search of food.

### Where do trout hide in rivers?

Take, for instance, salmon fly season on a freestone stream such as Rock Creek or the Big Blackfoot. During morning hours, trout will be congregated underneath the overhanging willows to catch the migration of huge stonefly nymphs, which make their way from mid-stream boulder to bank in order to climb ashore and emerge from their shucks. Come afternoon, though, when hatched bugs have begun their dive-bombing mating flights, big trout will often seek out long mid-river bubble-seams to gorge on egg-laying, hummingbird-size chunks of protein. Toward the evening, these same fish will seek out eddies where the dead or crippled bugs are still swirling around and have not yet been washed downstream. The old saying "Fish where the fish are" should be modified: "Fish where the food is, and the fish will be there."

### What about shade or undercut banks?

Similar "food-induced trout migrations" occur throughout the season in myriad ways on myriad rivers. My personal favorite is the "Smith River Earthworm Gumbo Feed," which happens each year during early season runoff on the Smith, when the water is the color of a macchiato. This time of year the river runs big, and often flows over grass islands, displacing earthworms. Trout know that such food is extremely vulnerable (worms can wiggle but can't swim like a minnow) and protein-rich, so they literally nose up into the grass, sometimes in six inches of water, and open their mouths to the surge of worms. It's commonplace to catch a trout that literally vomits up a gob of worms into the bottom of your boat.

In general, the biggest trout generally occupy the most ideal lies in the river, holding spots that put fish in the prime spot to get the most food with the least amount of effort. Overall, trout will take refuge under cutbanks, near downed trees, in front of and behind boulders, under choppy water, alongside cliffs, in weeds, rip-rap constructed of old cars half a century ago, on color changes, amongst other fish—ultimately, a trout will take cover anywhere it can.

Trout take cover to hide from direct sunlight, but mostly from predators, the list of which does not exclude trout. From the time they are fry, trout learn that danger—in the form of birds, crayfish, raccoons, other fish, even strange alien-like water beetles—abounds. I have seen 6-inch fish eaten by 14-inch fish, and I have seen 14-inch fish eaten by 22-inch fish. There is a long-faded picture in a fly shop in Missoula of a bull trout that attempted to eat a 20-inch cutthroat—both fish died, of suffocation and trauma, respectively. This is all to say that the ratio of predator size to prey size can be surprisingly small. The angler pitching an 8-inch streamer might catch a 10-inch trout or a coveted 2-footer.

Perhaps more threatening to trout than trout, though, are birds of prey, such as kingfisher, osprey, eagle, etc. It is because of these birds' sharp beaks and claws that trout flee your noisy, botched cast so quickly, and it's why guides in New Zealand won't allow their clients to fish with bright fly lines—because trout are constantly attuned to shadows, flicks of light, anything out of ordinary that occurs from above.

## What about saltwater fish? Do they need the same things as trout?

Saltwater fish, incidentally, such as bonefish and redfish, are equally sensitive. However, in terms of cover, freshwater trout generally need more cover than saltwater species of fish that frequent shallow water, or "the flats," to feed. These fish spend most of their time schooled up in deeper blue water (cover, of sorts) and move onto shallow water expanses in conjunction with tidal events to feed heavily. It is on the flats where these fish are most susceptible to birds of prey, as well as sharks and barracuda: danger.

When on the flats, these sensitive fish become hypersensitive. A bonefish feeding its way across a shallow flat recalls a cat burglar: a creature with intense purpose and care with one thing in mind—don't get caught! I recall stalking a large bonefish on foot once in the Florida Keys for what seemed like an hour. It was hard work walking quietly but quickly across the flat, and when I finally got within casting distance of the ten-pound fish, I took my hat off to wipe the sweat off my forehead. The movement of my arm to my head was enough to send the fish packing for the Marquesas!

The lesson here is simple: It takes a lot of work not to spook a fish, and not much ineptitude to spook one. In the Keys, where anglers have pursued flats species passionately for over half a century, fish have "adapted" to worry about nearly everything in their environment, to the extent that the traditional "overhead" cast has been replaced by a side-arm cast called "the gooch," which aims the fly high over the fish so that it settles not with a plop but with a dimple.

### How do I keep from spooking a fish?

Knowing that fish are innately attuned to danger, the best anglers present themselves and their fly as undetectably as possible. Many anglers make a practice of wearing drab-colored clothing, but the crazies wear camouflage. Tons of anglers will buy an olive fly line instead of a fluorescent yellow one, but the real obsessed folks actually sand their fly rod down to take the glare off the graphite's finish, rub mud on their leader so that it doesn't shine too brightly. I even know an old guide in Michigan who ties his flies only on stainless steel black hooks because traditional steel hooks get too shiny in the cedar-stained tanic rivers of the upper Midwest.

Again, one can never be too precautious when it comes to pursuing a quarry whose entire being is bent on survival. In this case, obsession is healthy.

When guiding, or simply observing other anglers on the river, I see mostly anglers who move too quickly and too loudly. Often, while wade fishing, I'll watch a client spot and walk toward a rising fish they could easily cast to from where they stand. "Where are you going?" I'll ask. "You can reach that fish from where you're standing." If you don't have to pound the ground with your feet to reach your quarry, by all means avoid it. Make fewer false casts, and whenever possible, make your false casts away from the targeted fish before presenting the fly. Try not to be noticed.

In the end, the most effective anglers fully immerse themselves in their surroundings. As I will detail in the next chapter, "presentation" isn't just the final laying of one's fly on the water. It's an act that integrates the whole process—from costume, to observation, to approach, to cast, to mend, all the way through hooking, fighting, and landing the fish.

# Expert Advice: Russell Parks

## Reading Water

*The Missoulian Angler Fly Shop*
Missoula, Montana
www.missoulianangler.com

Russell's early days of fly fishing go back to the lakes of East Texas, where angling for bass with a fly rod was not very "fashionable," you might say. Russell made it to Missoula at the end of 1999 and quickly realized this was home. Developing the finesse for fishing small flies to picky trout came much later for Parks. After completing graduate work in Ohio, where finding trout was difficult yet possible, Russell found the local waters within minutes of downtown Missoula made staying an easy decision. Russell's career in outdoor and therapeutic recreation provided him the opportunity to expose people of all ages to the unique challenges and experiences wilderness settings have to offer. Now the owner of The Missoulian Angler Fly Shop, he hopes to use this background and develop it into a friendly, high-quality, customer-oriented business that consistently produces for its clients.

*In this chapter we are going to talk about reading the water. Do you think most anglers know what that means?*

Many anglers that come into the shop know how to read water but often miss the critical chapters of the area they are reading. Just like a good book, everyone reads it differently and those that look at it critically understand the subtle differences and how it is all related.

*How would you define reading the water?*
Looking at the river, creek, or lake and being able to systematically distinguish where the fish habitat might be.

*When you first came west and eventually to Montana, did you find that the amount of water available to fish was a little overwhelming?*
Absolutely. There was so much to fish, it certainly got in the way of the job search!

*How important was being able to read water in learning to fish Montana waters AND then having success?*
I fished a lot of water nobody in their right mind would fish . . . and I'm not talking about those difficult-to-reach "secret" spots. I fished everywhere there was water and got tired of spending hours on the water for a few fish in certain areas. Once I learned where the fish were, it became easier for me to cover those areas and move on.

*Explain some important things about reading the water? What do some people overlook?*
Anglers need to ask one specific question: Where is the water moving differently? These areas of inconsistent flows are where to concentrate your casts. If it is fast water, find the slow pockets or current seams. If it is slow, look for the shelter areas or where water might flow differently below the surface. I think the structure of the river bottom itself, and how it affects the flow, is commonly overlooked.

*Briefly explain what people should look for when they are staring at a stream.*
Think about why the fish would want to be there. You know they want to eat, and they want it to be easy to get food. Look for those

areas that are arranged nicely for trout to hold and feed in. An obvious one is behind rocks, but don't overlook the nice pillow in front of the rocks. Identify the riffles, edges of riffles, deep versus shallow areas, any structure like logs or rocks below the surface, swirling eddies, and remember to notice what the water is doing along the banks. I like to focus on any water that is coming into the run from a side channel or tributary also.

### What about depth of the water? How important is that?

Depth is always something to consider. Defining the shallow and deep portions of a run will allow you to focus on these areas appropriately. I like throwing the big junk down deep! Big streamers and nymphs dredging the depths for big fish! Okay, enough. Shallow riffles are fun to play in also, and certainly seem to hold more fish.

### What about clarity? Is that a concern?

How clear the river is will determine what flies, leaders, tippet, and approach you will use. Some days when the river is choco-late milk from warming spring temperatures, concentrating on the line just off the banks can produce some great fish. At this time of year, fish are hungry and holding in that little lane just waiting for your big stuff to float by. On the other hand, in those backwater sloughs, where monster hungry browns await sipping size 22s in crystal-clear spring water, the hackles up on the back of your neck tell you to get the long, thin leaders and tippet and start crawling commando behind the largest stem of a willow you can find along the bank. Yes, clarity can be a big factor, but don't be fooled. When your regular box won't get the job done on those cloudy water days, break out the bright-colored goofy flies that your eight-year-old niece tied for your last birthday. You might be sending her an order for a dozen more.

*Do you read water any differently based on the method you are fishing? Explain?*

Yes and no. When I *read* the water I'm getting the information necessary to know where the fish are. I will *fish* the water differently when drifting dries or dredging nymphs and streamers. Most of the time it is reading the water that determines what method of fishing I'll be doing.

*Explain the differences between pocket water, a slower run or spring creek/ tailwater run, and a riffle. Explain how an angler might target each of these.*

In my mind pocket water will run full of rocks and structures, which create little "pockets" of holding water for trout to linger behind, and often in front of. When fishing dry flies to pocket water, it is sometimes difficult to get a good, long drift without some creative antics with your rod and fly line. These pockets are full of multidirectional water flows that wreak havoc on your little fly and result in short, active drifts. Run your bug along the edges and let it drift down low in the pocket to be effective. Big, slashing strikes are not uncommon as the fish feels like it needs to take care of business in a hurry before the swirling water takes the food away again.

Slower runs create wonderful challenges. Gin-clear water with no riffles or movement means the fish have no filter between them and the bank where you just walked up. When you can spook away the fish of a lifetime simply by walking up or casting the line on the water, it doesn't take long to develop this love/hate relationship with the trout living in these runs. Pretty soon you are tripling your leader length, tying on spider wisps for tippet, tying on more specific patterns, and stalking Trout-zilla with the rod in your teeth. Finesse is the name of the game, finding the pattern fish are rising or feeding on, and casting along that line very carefully and cautiously. This is the time to get it all in a scoop; one cast, one bug, one careful set with the rod.

Areas where riffles are created make good holding spots for fish. In the hot summer months, I often concentrate on nymphing in these areas outside of the hatches. Find the "little holes" in the riffle—those spots where the water seems to change character in the middle or sides of the run. As a rule, slow water meeting fast water equals trout. Cast far enough upstream to allow your fly time to get in proper position within the water column, and aligned with the character "flaw" before dragging. Riffles are great areas to fish blind—cast where no obvious fish are rising—drifting through each lane multiple times before moving on to the next. A systematic approach to riffles will serve you well. Start in close and downstream from the honey hole and work up and out if you can. People often miss the dry-fly action in riffles. Look closely, then look again more carefully. Many people find it difficult to see the fish rising among the slight chop or tight riffles.

*What are some common mistakes people forget or overlook or do when reading water?*

I tend to see people being too hasty when reading a particular piece of water. In fact, people don't often break it down into pieces in the first place. Take the big picture and break it into bits that are easier to digest and you will be more successful. Spend more time looking before unknowingly wading right into the water on top of the fish. It is easier to catch them when they are not speeding away from you.

*Any techniques, tips, or phrases you use when explaining where trout might be?*

I use the term "seams" a lot. It seems that seams come up whenever I start pointing out water to clients. Most interruption in the water flow creates one type of seam or another. One tip I refer to often is regarding riseforms from surface feeding trout. Beginning anglers need to realize these rings move downstream. Casting above the rise will produce more fish than those shots right on top of where you last saw the ring.

*A lot of anglers, especially on tailwater rivers, talk about foam lines.*

Always pay particular attention to foam lines on the water. Bugs often pile up in the foam and are easy picking for trout. It is easier to see the rising fish and make your casts where the foam lines stretch out along smooth flowing tail outs. However, I see many anglers miss the swirling eddy foam line rises. I've spent many days with delighted anglers who, at first, did not believe me when I pointed out the rising fish along these areas. Only after reluctantly dropping the fly in, seeing nothing, and then lifting the rod on my "SET!" did they become true foam heads. Now they know: Foam is Home.

**Quick-Glance Summary:**

Look before you leap

Look for any water that is moving differently

Reading water determines what method to use

In off-colored water look for the seam just off the bank

Pocket-water fish hold in any break

In slower water be stealthy

In riffles look for the little holes

Look for the seams

Foam is home—look to foam lines for feeding fish

# Chapter Four

# Looks Can Kill

## Presentation. Getting Your Flies in the Spot and Looking Natural

### What is all this talk about mending and why is it so important?

When I find myself teaching a beginner how to fly fish for trout, the first thing I do is break a small stick or bud from a tree and throw it on the water. "Watch how that stick moves," I'll say. "See how it floats, unattached to anything. That's how we want to make your fly appear on the water: as if it's not attached to anything." Of course, this is easier said than done, since the fly is tied to a tippet that is tied to a leader that is tied to a fly line that is tied to backing that is fastened to a reel, etc. When folks say, "Drag-free drift," this is what they mean. Often, while guiding, I'll get a query from a nearby boat: "What are they biting on?" My answer is nearly always: "A drag-free drift," meaning that the presentation is far more important than the actual fly. As the saying goes, "It ain't the arrow, it's the archer."

In addition to being able to make a 50-foot straight line cast, the competent angler should be able to effectively manage his or her line once it's on—or just before it hits—the water. Above all, this means knowing how and when to "mend" one's line.

### How do I mend effectively?

A mend is a manipulation of the fly line by the rod that makes the overall presentation of the fly more effective. A mend can be a loop of line that gets tossed upstream so that the fly floats downstream without drag for longer; a mend can be a swath of slack line that is fed into

### Downstream Mend

The downstream mend is ideal when your fly lands in faster water and your fly line lands in slower water.

### Upstream Mend

Use this mend when your fly lands in slower water and your fly line is floating in faster water. Multiple mends may be required to achieve this. Veteran Missouri River guide Garrett Munson once said this about an upstream mend: Mend, mend again.

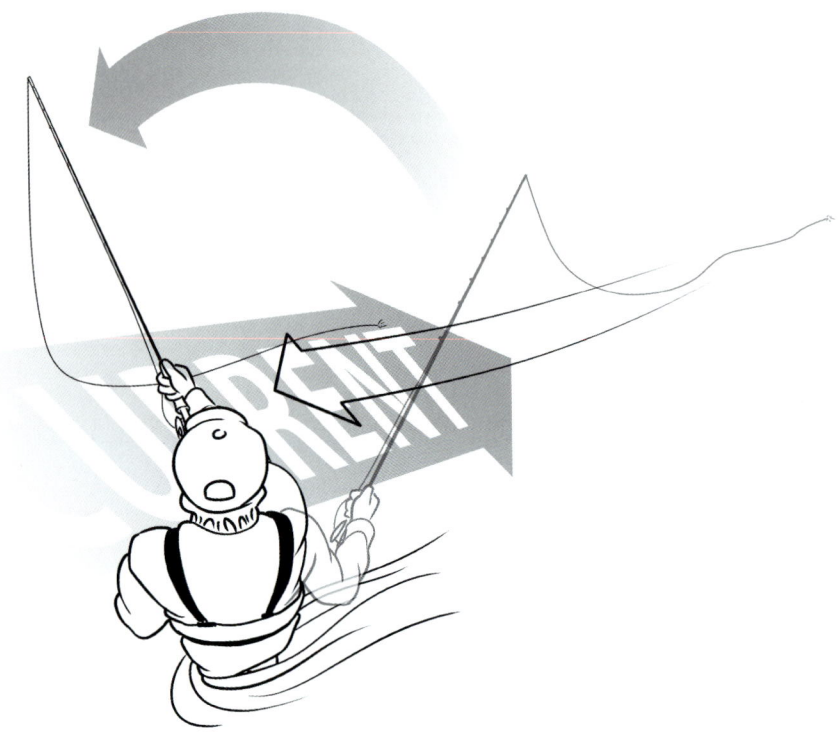

### Power Mend

Another name for this could be a "cast without a cast" mend. This mend is accomplished by raising the rod and fly line off the water and pulling the fly back into original line of drift or a new line of drift. Ideal when you have brush cover behind you or a ferocious upstream or downstream wind, and a full backcast and forward cast would cause greater problems.

the drift after a downstream cast; a mend can be a roll cast of slack line that allows nymphs to sink deeper; a mend can even be a downstream flick of line that makes a dead drifted streamer rise up off the bottom and look like a vulnerable crawfish or minnow to big trout, a deadly tactic on the lower Madison.

Overall, I will say this much for mending: In a boat, at least, I would much rather have a competent mender and line manager than I would a competent caster. Marginal casts can be compensated for with long, drag-free drifts; and only someone good at mending and managing line can make long drifts happen.

## What is "tracking" and why is it important?

Another thing good line managers do is "track" their fly and their line with the rod tip as it progresses downstream. Tracking is essential to ensuring optimal drift; in addition, it keeps the angler "at the ready," to set the hook. I love watching a good nymph fisherman, like my brother Carl, pick apart a run. If observed from above, the rod of a great nymph fisherman like Carl looks a lot like the hands on an old-fashioned stopwatch: The rod flicks line upstream then briskly follows its progression downstream to a given point, then stops and repeats the movement. If the line or the indicator so much as tilts to indicate a fish, the angler hauls back with a hook-set, preferably in a downstream direction. Tracking is keeping one's metaphorical finger on the pulse of the river.

## I don't need split shot, do I?

Generally speaking, in the world of nymph fishing, the better one is as a mender, the less split shot one needs to get his flies down to the fish. Do you need split shot to be an effective nymph fisherman? Even with the advent of tungsten flies, I'd say, yes, you do need to carry some split shot, especially for tailwaters like the Bighorn and the Missouri, where, at least during runoff, leaders might span 12, even 14, feet.

Much of the nymph fishing I do on freestones, however, is led by the dearly beloved "Pat's Rubberlegs," a stonefly imitation that isn't split shot but is wrapped in lead and chenille, the latter of which gets wet and turns the fly into a veritable depth charge. Get the flies down to your desired depth as quickly as possible, and keep them there as long as possible, is the best advice I could give a rookie nympher.

And even to the dry-fly purist, I would say: Carry some split shot anyway, since you never know when your favorite hatch might turn into an event under water (can anyone say "sunken hoppers"?).

## What about size or color? Are they really important?

Sunken hoppers, of course, are a rare necessity, which brings me to the most important word in presentation: priority. When making a fly selection, the angler generally must prioritize one imitation factor over another. By and large, what's most important to trout is the size and "profile" of the fly (that is, the impression the fly makes on the water), with color trailing a good ways behind, though not altogether irrelevant.

To elucidate, I'll reference the Trico spinner fall on a small river like the East Gallatin near my hometown of Bozeman. Natural Trico mayflies in the spent stage, sized #20–24, coat the water everywhere on an August morning. Their bodies are black and their wings clear, except for the females, which possess a cream-colored body with a black thorax and clear wings. In other words: small, barely visible specks of "mayfly dust" cover the surface of the water, and you, valiant angler, must come up with an imitation that appeases the steadily feeding brown trout tucked underneath the grass bank.

In this situation, as in many other similar situations, since the profile of the fly on the water is the most important distinguishing characteristic, the angler should choose a tiny fly with a thin body and spent wings that float flush in the surface film of the river. A heavily hackled fly such as an Elk Hair Caddis, even if it were the precise size of the naturals on the river, would fail to make an accurate impression on the water, and fish would refuse it.

What the angler must remember is that fish are always keying on one or two identifying characteristics of a fly—and profile is nearly always number one. Accuracy of size comes next—and it's worth noting that the smaller the fly, the greater discrepancies appear—but there is more wiggle room here, and of course, there are exceptions to these rules, as when a Trico-sipping trout decides to crush a size 10 black beetle pattern! Why would a smart trout do such a thing? Because it can!

## What about fly floatant or desiccant? Which ones are the best?

Back to the East Gallatin, though, where the trout are still rising. After catching a fish on your number 22 Trico spinner, you'll need to reapply some floatant to your fly. Gink is the famous silicone gel that has been usurped in recent years by Loon Company's Aquel. I generally apply a gel floatant to a dry fly before fishing it, and then, after a fish or two have been caught on the fly, apply a desiccant such as Frogs Fanny, Dry Shake, or Fly Duster. These powder-based products return the fly to its original buoyancy, and coat it with a nice powdery white hue. This aids visually when using small or dark flies, and keeps flies tied with CDC perky.

Probably because it creates less surface tension on the water, a high-floating fly nearly always catches the most fish. I also keep a tin of the old-fashioned Mucelin around for coating the last few feet of the fly line. But remember, you don't need a vest-load of fancy products to make a fly float high—you can always use your t-shirt to sponge off a fly, and lip balm doubles as fly floatant, though not vice versa!

## How do I rig for fishing nymphs?

After talking dry flies, it seems a bit sacrilegious to dovetail into a discussion on nymphs, but I will do so anyway—because I am a guide and I like to catch fish! Rule number one in nymphing is identify the food source and make a general match with a nymph or two. Sometimes this means choosing two different food sources—like a stonefly and a caddis pupa—or choosing a general imitation and a more exact one, like a pheasant tail and a blue-wing olive emerger. Rule number two is identify the depth at which fish are feeding. Usually this is at least halfway down the water column, although sometimes fish "nymph" very close to the surface. Then rig your leader so that the distance from the flies to your indicator is one and a half times the depth of the water you intend to fish.

From there, you're ready to go! Now the real work starts.

# Expert Advice: John Bailey

## Dry-Fly Fishing:
## Basics to Advanced Techniques and Gear

*Dan Bailey's Fly Shop*
Livingston, Montana
www.dan-bailey.com

John Bailey is the son of Dan Bailey, the founder of the legendary Dan Bailey's Fly Shop in Livingston, Montana. In 1938 the Bailey family moved from New York and opened the shop. As a kid John explored nearly every nook and cranny of the Livingston area. In grade school and into high school, John would marvel at the fishermen who would visit the store and the area and the broad geographic range from which they came. The store was always busy and John was always helping out. Even in the summers during college John would return to Livingston, excited with what new summertime fishing stories would be created. John gained his expertise by simply fishing from sunrise to sunup. Over time he just became pretty damn good at it. In the 1970s it became a full-time affair for John, and since then he's run the shop, expanded the business, and had a great time along the way. John cannot remember the first time he caught a fish on a dry fly, but he can certainly say he's caught many and enjoyed them all.

*What is the appeal of fishing with dry flies?*

First, you get to fish lots of different types of water. Second, you are usually sight fishing to rising fish. Third, if you are not sight fishing then you are at least blind casting to the various types of water or structure. You just get to see a lot of the action.

*As for fly lines, are you a double taper or weight-forward guy?*

Over the years I've liked the fact that you can shoot weight-forwards better, but on spring creeks I would use a double taper. Rods have gotten better as well, so a taper of the line is not as important as it used to be. A double taper has a different casting stroke, and there are times when I really like one, like when I am using my cane rods. To me casting is just so natural that I don't think much about fly lines.

*What about rods? Do you recommend a certain rod for dry-fly fishing?*

I'm pretty fussy about rods. So I buy one for a specific stream or purpose. I've got a lot of rods! My general fishing I use an 8½-foot five-weight. Rods have gotten a lot faster and I like that—I don't really like a softer tip rod for most situations, especially here in Livingston, which is known for wind. I grew up and learned with fishing cane and I still fish cane a lot today. There were years and years I only used cane rods. I want a rod that I can really lean into and use all of the rod, and the desire to use all of the rod goes right back to my being used to cane rod that bends all the way.

*What about a rod for a beginner or someone's first rod?*

What I've learned with people is that you've got to let them cast the rods. Everybody has a little bit different style or stroke or the way they handle their body. If you try various rods when you are learning, you will find one that works for you. There will be a rod that will match your stroke, unless you've got basic problems with your stroke.

*First, we are talking mostly about dry-fly fishing on freestone rivers and faster, smaller creeks and rivers. How might you differentiate between a freestone and a tailwater?*

A freestone will have a very different set of tactics than fishing a spring creek or a tailwater. Most of the fishing that I will talk about will be for fishing freestones. In general we fish a shorter leader, we are not concerned about finesse, and we look at making more and shorter drifts than longer drifts that might occur on a tailwater. The other chapters in the book should cover, more in-depth, fishing tailwaters and spring creeks.

*What about any other specialized equipment that you would recommend?*

I use an 8½ five-weight on the Yellowstone or Boulder. If I go to flat water or a spring creek, that's not what I'm using. I'd use a longer rod, like 9-foot three-weight. I'm using much lighter rods because I'm using much smaller flies and longer leaders.

*So would you say an angler should have an arsenal of rods for fishing dry flies?*

Yes, if you fish a lot of water. Most people only fish one stream most of the time. But things have changed with rods. The newer rods make it so one rod can handle more situations. They've refined the actions with graphite and now you can cast a hopper on the same rod that you can cast a size 20 Parachute Adams.

*What about any other specialized equipment or gear you recommend?*

Leaders. Leaders are the forgotten thing about rigging your tackle. They get very little respect, but deserve the utmost attention. You have to transfer the energy from the fly line to the fly. There are so many different situations in dry-fly fishing—small mountain streams with fast water, large windy rivers, spring creeks. People just don't pay much attention to leaders and they should.

*What are some crucial factors in determining what leaders to use in a given situation?*

They need to have bigger butt sections. That will help transfer the energy better to get rid of a hinge. In flat water or on a spring creek, I will use a 12–15-foot leader. Otherwise I am using a 9- or 10-foot leader. For dry-fly fishing on a larger river, I would never use anything shorter than a 9-foot leader. And spend some decent money on leaders. Folks will have a $600 rod, a $300 reel, but buy the cheaper leader on the rack.

*Do you have a special fly floatant—do you like a liquid floatant or desiccant?*

For most situations I use a gel like Gink or Aquel. For bigger dries like salmon flies I will use a paste. When the dry fly gets slimed by the fish or the weeds, a drying powder helps a lot. Floatant and powders have come a long way since I began fishing and there has been a huge improvement. For little dries I use a powder all the time.

*Are you a proponent of a certain knot?*

Everybody thinks I am crazy for this, but I use a turle knot for all of my dries. The reason is the way the knot comes out the hook is always in line with the leader. In the past a turle knot would not have been as strong, but with the new leader material it is just as strong. I remember on the spring creeks I would watch a fish rise to my specific fly and the fish would get hooked. Well, I'd bring the fly in and with a little dry fly, size 18-22, the fly would cock funny with a slip or clinch knot. With a turle knot I know the leader is in line, and I know what my fly is doing. I want to eliminate as many variables as possible, and by knowing which way fly is floating on my tippet, that makes me more successful. I just know that the presentation is better.

*That brings us to the next big aspect of dry-fly fishing, and that is presentation. Do most anglers truly understand presentation?*

Not really. It all starts with your drift. And around here we have so much water that there are so many different techniques that people use. For instance I've watched a lot of anglers fish and so many times they cast and the drift they start is already a failed drift. Many people make drifts that are too long. If they would just shorten the drift, especially on faster waters, they will have more drifts and each drift will have a better chance. The faster the water, the shorter the drift. The slower the water, the longer the drift. For me I tend to cover a lot of water when I fish. My dad used to say, "Keep moving until you find a dumb fish."

*Anglers talk a lot about presentation. How do you feel about presentation versus exact imitation?*

Are you talking about the cast or flies?

*Mostly concerning the fly on the water.*

I do a lot more fishing with flies that are general than specific to a bug or a bug's life during a hatch. When you get into tailwater or spring creeks, you have to be somewhat close to what the hatch is, but generally why was the Royal Wulff the biggest selling fly for decades? The same could be said for the Prince Nymph or Elk Hair Caddis. All of those patterns have things in them that look like natural bugs, and it triggers an instinct in the fish to eat. Here is another way to look at it: When looking at fly boxes you'd see someone's from back East who all winter can't fish so they are inside tying flies and creating all these exact imitations, and their fly box is stuffed with all sorts of interesting creations. Or someone's from Montana who can't afford to buy flies but just tied them to catch fish because they were too busy fishing and wanted ones that just looked bushy and buggy.

*Would you say presenting a fly that looks like anything they may have eaten in the past week is better than something that is exact to what is hatching?*

On a spring creek it may or a tailwater it may. On those waters you have unique hatches and lots of those bugs. On a freestone like the Yellowstone or Rock Creek or Boulder, you just don't know exactly what they are eating that day. Take for example the Mother's Day caddis on the Yellowstone. There are lots and lots of caddis on the water, and if you don't see YOUR fly, you will miss a strike. Seeing your fly becomes the most important aspect in choosing a dry fly. One of the biggest selling dry flies is the Parachute Adams.

*What would you tell a beginner about dry-fly fishing if you are guiding them on a day when fishing dries will be the most effective way to fish?*

When wading, I watch a lot of anglers that fish and their fly is downstream of them, but they haven't learned their problem. When they turn upstream and start fishing, they don't know what to do with that line coming at them. They set themselves up to where half the time the fly is ineffective. They need to cast more often. On faster-moving streams they need to fish more upstream and at a slight angle across the stream, not straight out in front of them. Things are happening fast, and they need to use their line hand and rod hand working together to keep that fly floating. A lot of that can start by just casting at a slightly upstream angle. Set the odds in your favor by casting at a better upstream angle and getting your hand dexterity down.

*What are some observations you have about anglers that have fished for several years but only fish ten or so days a year? They are not beginners, but they are not experts.*

If they have a problem, it is usually because they are fishing dries on a piece of water they are not used to fishing. Most people fish the same water most of the time. Growing up here, we learn to adjust to different types of water. Those anglers can either watch other people to see what they are doing, hire a guide, or spend more time and learn the newer water. Some of it can be as simple as just fly selection. For example, if you are on the Gallatin, a river that is really fast and very unique in nature, if you don't pick up and cast right away, you are in trouble. Unless you've done that you will have trouble.

*If someone is coming out to Montana from the upper Midwest or the South and wants to fish a mountain stream, what would you tell them?*

If you let them watch you for a bit, they will probably pick it up. They should learn by observation. If they hire a guide, that helps but if they just watch and observe how other anglers are fishing, that will help as well. You can also watch and see where the hatches are coming off because that is where all the people are! But also don't get too hung up on local streams and local habits. Folks will come out with some weird fly from back home and it catches lots of fish.

*For learning various dry-fly fishing techniques, would you say observation is key?*

Absolutely. In dry-fly fishing, fish are going to come to the surface. In different bodies of water, fish hold in different areas. For example for hopper fishing, and hoppers are not a hatch, the hoppers land back in the water and the fish are in totally different spots than they are for caddis or salmon flies. For caddis the fish will be in riffles, for salmon flies the fish will be along the banks. If you've been around a place you know the things, if you don't you have to observe—and that's one of the fun things about going new places.

*What about what any techniques anglers should really master if they want to be successful in any situation?*

In addition to observation, I observe what other people fish. People almost always fish something different than what I would fish. And a lot of times they catch fish where I would never catch fish. So, am I always right? You should always be willing to try something new! I know what works well a lot, but I pass up stuff that I know contains fish. I may think, "Boy, that is a wasted cast," and boy, they catch a fish and I have to laugh at myself. But we all do that. Just because it didn't work before, you just maybe ought to try that. Getting that experience and being good in every situation just takes time and practice. But in time everyone finds their enjoyment—some people are natural casters and love to cast, some just like to wander around and catch a few fish, some just like to look at the scenery and let the day pass. Well you know, experts typically say, "Dah-dah-dah, this way, not that way." Well, that works a lot, but I say try your other ideas as well and be open to other ideas as well.

*With dry-fly fishing does it help to be flexible and not rigid in how you fish?*

Well, you need to be that in all fishing. Pressure these days can dictate that—if you have a lot of wading anglers or a lot of boats floating by or people in your usual type of water.

*How might you adjust to a crowded situation?*

Look to fish water that others may have missed. If in a boat, get out and stop a lot. There is always a piece of water that has not been fished.

*Do you have any mends, stripping techniques, or dealing with slack that you use?*

I will sometimes fish with my left hand if I am on a bank that is easier to fish it with my left. I may have to be tight on the bank, holding willows or using my right hand to keep balance. Or if I am in a boat and it is easier for me and the other angler, I will cast with my left hand. I'm not great at it, but sometimes it really helps me get my fly in more spots. As for mending, I mend seldom because I cast a lot. In a boat I mend a lot. I reach cast a lot, especially while in a boat.

*There are a lot of different names for various casts. How do you term a reach cast?*

I call it a reach mend or an in-the-air mend. When I fish, my arm is all over the place. I tell people that and I encourage that. When I am wade fishing, I reach cast some and even more in slower water like on a tailwater or spring creek. In faster water it is back to shorter drifts and more casts—you know boom, boom, boom, drift, drift, drift.

*What about slack in dry-fly fishing? Good thing, bad thing, both?*

Terrible. Especially on freestones. If you get up to slower water or spring creek-ish water, you might want a little more slack because of the slower currents and in the different currents you may want more slack or some S curves in the fly line. You will get a little longer float over those various currents. Otherwise slack only causes you to miss a strike or strike too hard. I sometimes tell folks to fish with their left hand over their right so they won't strike so hard! For many beginners they don't even think about managing slack or floating that dry fly; so many of them are just happy they got the fly out there! During the filming of *A River Runs Through It* I taught them on the ponds for a bit, then we went out to the river and all of a sudden we had this new problem. Dealing with line management and floating the dry float is crucial, and getting that slack out or having just the right amount is so crucial, and a lot people don't talk about it enough.

*How can drag help or hurt you?*

It can help you during a caddis hatch when you want to have a moving fly—there are times when a dry fly goes just under the surface and the fish will take. And in that instance it is really not drag since you are causing that to occur. A lot of drag goes back to setting up that good drift initially. Everybody wants to cast too far. Reel in some line, try more drifts, shorter casts, and that might solve it. With these newer rods most anglers are surprised that a shorter cast will work just as good as a longer cast because you get the fly to float how you want it. That allows me to just pick up and re-cast, which keeps my fly in the spot longer so I have less false casts.

*In Montana we like to consider caddis, mayflies, stoneflies, and terrestrials as the main bugs that would float on the surface. What would be your favorite fly pattern for each of these?*

*Caddis:* Elk Hair Caddis. Easy to see and buggy.

*Mayflies:* An Adam's, and I like a Parachute Adams because you can see it.

*Stoneflies:* There are a few sizes of stoneflies, but an Elk Hair salmon fly. Something big and bushy so you can see it in big water.

*Terrestrials:* For hoppers foam seems to be the trend and it works really well. You can twitch it and it gives great action.

*What about some things you look for in a given pattern?*

Peacock herl. It just has a certain quality that looks buggy. Red catches the light. Peacock and red are wonderful things to have in a dry fly.

*What about your favorite dry fly that you always have in your box—the one fly you wouldn't be caught dead without?*

Royal trude. I don't use it as much as I should, but it is very effective. I use it a lot in low-light conditions. It's got white. It's got peacock and red. It's a downwing, meaning the big wing lays flat. If it gets under the water, fish take it.

*Are you a believer in that you fish dries most of the time or only when you see enough fish rising?*

A lot depends on the time of year. A big change in recent years has been to fish the double rig, a big dry and nymph trailing tied to the big dry. I hope that the fish are eating the dry more. Late in the summer I am going to fish hoppers. During the salmon fly hatch, I am going to fish salmon flies. When you know a river, you know if dries will work on a given day. On spring creeks and tailwaters, you need to observe more, but you also know by time of year too. So often some weird adjustment to your fly, like coloring the body black or clipping the hair, will work, especially with dry flies, and will catch fish.

*How do you sum all of this up?*

If you get so dialed in, if you don't think about it, you've quit exploring the fishing on a given day. You must be flexible to continue to try new things and change, especially when it comes to fishing dry flies. Those who do have the desire to explore come up with new patterns or a different time of day to fish, and all of a sudden they are successful. Over the years I've learned to fish a lot more water because I've watched how other people do it and where they've had fish eat a dry fly where I would overlook. I know a lot of guides who tell their clients "just let your fly drag across the river here as I row across" and often they catch a fish.

*What is your last piece of advice for dry-fly fishing?*

First is that what we've talked about is mostly about dry-fly fishing on freestone rivers and smaller mountain streams. Dry-fly fishing on tailwater is a very different world than, say, fishing salmon flies on the Yellowstone. With that said anglers need to be flexible during all their dry-fly fishing, and watch that slack!

**Quick-Glance Summary:**

Spring creeks: double taper fly line

Other waters: weight-forward fly line

Windy rivers use a faster rod

Leaders are crucial

Shorter, more accurate drifts

General imitation rather than specific match

When wading, angle your cast upstream

Learn by observation

Be flexible in your fishing

# Chapter Five

# Faking It

## Choosing the Right Flies and
## Using Them at the Right Times

### Why should I care about nymphs?

Unlike many anglers, I was not born a dry-fly snob. Growing up in Bozeman near the Madison and Gallatin Rivers and the experienced fly fishermen who plied those waters, I learned the old adage early: 90 percent of a trout's diet does indeed exist underneath the surface of the water. As a youngster, I didn't have many flies, but I would never venture out without a few Prince Nymphs and Hare's Ears. True, dry-fly fishing is generally more exciting than nymphing, but the practical angler knows that the rent gets paid down deep in the water column. It's not that fish can't usually find food on the surface of the water—it's

just that there's generally more food downstairs, and it's safer and more efficient for trout to eat down there in the shadows, beneath the refractive surface of the water.

Also, while trout don't have microscopic calculators in their heads, they are genetically imprinted to constantly consider the following ratio: calories expended vs. calories earned. If you were a trout, would you rise to slurp an adult stonefly and risk getting whopped on the head by an osprey when you could eat an equally nutritious stonefly nymph in the safety and shade of a cutbank?

Since nymphs and larva (mayfly, stonefly, caddis, midges, damselflies, etc.) are consistently available to trout, they make up the bulk of a trout's diet. Furthermore, there are scores of protein-rich food items—aquatic red worms, leeches, scuds, freshwater shrimp, minnows, fry, crawfish, etc.—that live only underwater. Often times while guiding the Missouri River during runoff, when the grass banks and islands are underwater, I have numerous clients catch the largest brown trout of their angling career on aquatic worm imitations—these huge fish had bellies shaped like Dunlop footballs and were literally regurgitating worms in the net.

That's why you should care about nymphs.

### What is the difference between an emerger and an adult?

Aquatic insects have dynamic, multistage life cycles, and trout key on these various stages at various times of the day and the season. Each bug—be it a caddis, a mayfly, a midge, a damselfly, or a stonefly—has a bottom-crawling nymphal stage, an emergent stage, an adult stage, and a spent stage. The angler wishing to capitalize on the fish's most gluttonous periods of feeding should learn these stages and their most effective imitations.

Take the Western Green Drake, for instance, a storied hatch on Rocky Mountain freestone waters. The Green Drake nymph is an extremely adept crawler, clambering over bowling-ball-size boulders for most of the year, until the water temperature and accumulated hours of sunlight tells the bug it's time to hatch. At this time—mid-June to mid-July depending on the elevation of the stream—the mayfly nymphs release their holds on the boulders and make for the surface of the water, where they rapidly discard their nymphal shuck and "sprout" their wings. This stage (when the bug is caught in the surface film) is called the emergent stage.

It is during this husk-shucking emergent stage that trout can catch emergent insects "with their pants down" and can gorge before the insects' wings dry and the bugs become airborne. For this reason, experienced anglers live for humid, even drizzly days, when hatching insects are vulnerable for longer. Some of my most memorable fishing days in recent memory, in fact, have occurred early or late in the season, on drizzly March and November days, when the hatching Blue-Winged Olives on the Missouri seemed glued to the river's surface and the big rainbows fed with storybook rhythm and abandon.

## What is all this talk about "cripples"?

A cripple is a deformed or injured mayfly. During their hatching something went wrong in their development; therefore, they cannot fly away. Unfortunate for the insects, but fortunately for us and for trout these bugs are more easily eaten off the surface. Generally, I match this small (size 18-22) hatching mayfly with a pattern that has a trailing "shuck" and hangs low in the water. These types of flies are often called "cripples," and one of the most dependable cripple patterns over the past two decades has been Quigley's Cripple, a fly whose rear half rides under the water while its front half floats. This fly's "posture" perfectly mimics a hatching mayfly's posture and says "come and get me" to the fish.

While guiding and fishing, I employ dozens of other "cripple" patterns—some call them stillborns, knock-downs, or film-riders—to help fool picky fish. Often, while fishing the Pale Morning Dun hatch, I'll watch hatching duns (adults) float by with their gray wings up, blonde bodies flat, and rusty brown shuck dragging below them in the water. In such instances, a bicolored fly pattern is a must. If you find yourself fishing over "rising" fish that won't take your dry fly, watch to see if the risers are actually taking the adult bugs, or if the fish are keyed on something "in the film"—this is often the case with the biggest, most technical fish.

## Do I really need to match the hatch?

The short answer is yes. The long answer is no.

I consider myself lucky to live in a state with diverse trout fishing opportunities. In Montana, as in many western states, trout flourish in freestones such as the Yellowstone, tailwaters such as the Bighorn, spring creeks such as DePuy's, and stillwaters such as Georgetown Lake. Each type of water requires a different type of approach if one is to be successful at fooling trout. Generally speaking, the slower, clearer, and flatter the water, the more exact one must be with an imitation when matching the hatch; the rowdier the water, the more suggestive or impressionistic one can be.

During the yellow sally stonefly hatch on the riffle-filled Yellowstone, for instance, I might pound the banks with a size 12 yellow Trude (a bushy, buoyant fly with a white calf-tail wing) to great success. The same hatch on the slower, glassier Bighorn, however, will require fishing a lower-riding, subtler pattern, perhaps something with a CDC wing and thin rubber legs, if my clients and I are to be productive.

## Why should I care about size and color?

As I stated earlier, during a hatch, I always try to match my flies to the naturals' profile, size, and color—in that order. Size (paramount) and color (far from priority, though Gary LaFontaine's "Color Attraction Theory" is worth investigating) speak for themselves, but profile is a more nuanced "quality" that refers to the impression the natural bug makes on the water—an adult mayfly's wings look like a sailboat, for example, while an adult caddis's look like a tent.

Many experienced anglers would argue that profile or impression is the most important quality to imitate. And finally, matching the behavior of the naturals is very important. During a yellow sally egg-laying flight, for instance, the naturals often skitter across the surface of the water, eliciting violent strikes from feeding trout; dead-drifted imitation will induce some strikes, but a twitched fly will have them banging heads to get at the bug.

When arriving on the river, I peruse the shallows and bankside spider webs, as well as the air above the water, to see what types of insects are available to the trout. Keeping in mind that the most visible insect is often the "masking hatch," some anglers I know carry small aquarium nets, or stomach pumps, to help them discover exactly what trout are keyed in on.

There are, of course, exceptions to this advice, but as a guiding buddy of mine often says, "You know what fly the trout always eat? The one that floats like the naturals."

### Why is a Stimulator a great dry fly?

A "Stimulator" is a high-riding, heavily hackled dry fly developed a few decades ago by Randall Kauffman to imitate the giant stonefly, or salmon fly, hatch, in California. The fly's elk hair wing makes the bug buoyant and visible—a perfect searching fly for riffly water, or for matching the hatch when stoneflies abound. Tied in smaller sizes, the Stimulator is a serviceable caddis imitation, as well as a good yellow sally match. The fly can be twitched, sunk, and fished on the swing, or dead drifted. Often, when spent caddis or small stones are present, I'll clip the hackle off the bottom of a Stimulator so the fly floats flush in the surface film.

Simply because it *suggests* something big and juicy to the trout—it could be a moth, a giant caddis or sedge, or even a small mouse wading

across the river—a Stimulator is a good dry fly. Other great suggestive "pork chops" include John Perry's Bugmeister and Brent Taylor's
Fat Albert. Like the Stimulator, these bugs can be fished in myriad
sizes and colors, twitched, dragged, or dead-drifted through almost
any water type, and will induce strikes.

### What are the ten best trout flies?

Listing the ten best trout flies is a task as impossible as listing the ten
best albums of all time, or the ten best beers, or the ten most beautiful
women. To say the least, the list shifts with the maker's daily moods
and preference. LaFontaine's Emergent Sparkle Pupa, for instance,
wasn't in my top ten until the other night when I used it to catch a
dozen otherwise uncatchable healthy browns from a grassy bend on
the East Gallatin and recalled the fly's versatility.

But if I were given only one fly box for the rest of my life and
it was filled with only ten patterns of my choice, I would demand
the following:

1. **Parachute Adams**—This highly visible
   variation of the Lee Halladay classic
   can be fished in sizes 22-10 and works
   as a serviceable match for nearly every
   adult stage of mayfly; it could be a
   floating nymph stuck in the film, or a
   fully hatched dun, or a spent spinner.
   With a sharp pair of fly-tying scissors

   on hand, further modifications can be made to the fly while on
   the stream—a snip in the front of the parachute hackle will give
   the bug a more realistic down-wing spinner appearance, and I've
   even watched a friend peel the hackle off the fly, sink it with a
   split shot, and fish it successfully as an emerging PMD nymph.
   Skittered, the fly also passes for a cranefly or an egg-laying stone.

2. **Elk Hair Caddis**—A Montana-born fly, this Al Toth creation is nearly as versatile as the Parachute Adams. Heavily hackled, made extremely buoyant by its elk-hair wing, the fly floats well through even the most hard-charging riffles. It can be twitched to imitate an ovipositing  caddis, swung on a tight line to imitate an emerging caddis, and (especially with clipped hackle) fished on a dead drift to imitate a spent caddis. In the West, where caddis are players from mid-May through October, this isn't an imitation you want to be without. Heck, I've even caught steelhead on this fly!

3. **Bugmeister**—Another Montanan, the Bugmeister was invented by Rock Creek guru John Perry after his clients caught dozens of fish on a trashed Royal Wulff. His original creation utilized lots of peacock herl, an elk-hair wing, a synthetic parachute, and lots of grizzly hackle,  but variations (even purple and pink) abound. Like the Elk Hair Caddis, this fly can be twitched or dead-drifted to imitate stoneflies and caddis. While I've had great days fishing it during yellow sally hatches, my favorite time to fish it is during the giant golden stonefly emergence on the Missouri and lower Yellowstone. The solitary big browns beg for this fly when it's tied with a burgundy body.

4. **Quigley's Cripple**—Originally tied to imitate an emerging or crippled mayfly, this bug is perhaps the best we have at representing an insect that is trapped in the water's surface film. Tied with a pheasant tail body and a dubbed thorax that sit under the water, and a parachute hackle and deer hair wing  that float atop, the fly is a dead-ringer for mayflies at their most vulnerable stage (just remember to apply floatant to only the front half of the bug). It can also be twitched during a caddis emergence to elicit thunderous strikes.

5. **Pheasant Tail**—The tale of the Pheasant Tail begins with English River-Keeper Frank Sawyer, who tied this fly to imitate baetis nymphs on English chalk streams. Sawyer used copper wire to rib and subtly weight the fly, and beef up the thorax in order to mimic the tear-drop shape of mayfly nymphs.  The initial Americanized variation of Sawyer's nymph saw clipped pheasant tail added to suggest legs, and myriad variations have ensued. From bead-head to crystal flash bubble-back, the Pheasant Tail has perhaps more incarnations than any other fly out there. Though I'll fish all of these variations, I'm a Pheasant Tail purist of sorts, preferring the more understated original—fished 6 inches underneath a Parachute Adams, there isn't a more dependable fly for tricky sippers.

6. **Bead-Head Prince**—When I first started fly-fishing, I rarely went through a day without tying this fly on. My dry-fly purist buddies would ridicule me, but my bent rod would chide them right back. In smaller sizes, this bug works well to imitate dislodged caddis cases and stonefly nymphs, and in larger sizes its split goose-biot tail suggests big stoneflies. I've even used it on the Big Hole in a size 22 to match sunken Trico spinners!

7. **Pat's Rubber Legs**—I've heard this variation of the Girdle Bug referred to as "The Pickle," "Cat Turd," "Pig Sticker," etc., and whatever you call it, it's simply the most effective stonefly nymph imitation ever invented. Its lead wraps and chenille body make it sink like a rock, and its multiple rubber legs titillate big trout literally twelve months out of the year. In addition to being a stonefly nymph imitation nonpareil, it also makes a great crawdad, cranefly larva, October caddis hut, etc. On the Blackfoot during runoff, I'll fish it on the dead drift, the twitch, even the jig.

8. **Olive Wooly Bugger**—Another incredibly versatile fly, I've fished this fly in sizes as small as #14 or as big as #2—½ inch to 6 inches long—and caught big fish on it all over the world. It's a great leech imposter, as well as a dynamite minnow imitation, cranefly larva match (strip it faster than a jackrabbit  on crack!), and dead-drifted it will pass for a stonefly, too. Give me life, liberty, and a 2/0 Olive Wooly Bugger on the Missouri in November—or give me death!

9. **San Juan Worm**—Ahem. Many will debate this fly's "flyness," but few will argue its prowess with the trout. Aquatic red worms exist in nearly every stream, and earthworms find their way into the water column nearly every day. One hundred percent pure protein, incredibly vulnerable in the 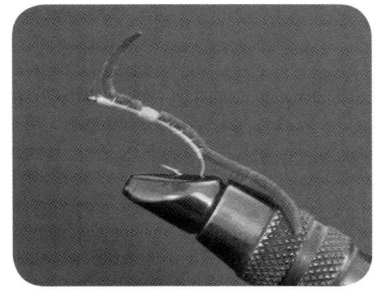 water, worms require very little effort for trout to catch and yet provide extreme nutrient level. The original San Juan Worm was tied on the San Juan River to imitate this rich tailwater's aquatic red worms, but the bug and its infinite variations work extremely well on freestones, too.

10. **Morrish's Hopper**—In the West, a guide won't be caught with fewer than a dozen grasshopper imitations in his fly box, but if forced to choose one, I'd go with the Moorish's Hopper because this low-profile foam bug also strongly suggests a big golden stonefly, especially the nocturnal version that 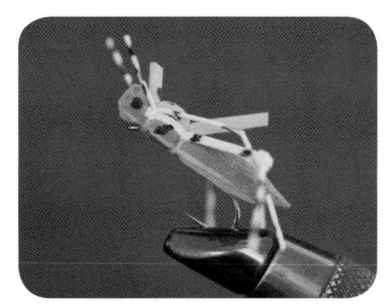 emerges on big freestone streams late in the summer. Twitched, dead-drifted, even stripped, the Moorish's works because its legs kick and stall exactly like a real grasshopper's legs—fished tight to the bank, or out in the long foam lines and tailouts, this bug has found its way into the maws of some very big brown trout in the past few years.

# Expert Advice: Steve Summerhill

## Nymph Fishing: Basic to Advanced Skills and Gear

*The Rivers Edge*
Bozeman, Montana
www.theriversedge.com

Steve Summerhill is the co-owner of the Rivers Edge fly shop in Bozeman, Montana. Steve grew up in Alaska fly-fishing at the age of six. He built his first rod when he was eight years old. For college Steve chose Montana, and he poked and prodded nearly every piece of water in southwest Montana. Upon moving to Montana, he  realized trout fishing here was quite a bit different than Alaska—no longer would any color egg pattern work! After a few years of college, Steve began guiding and from that point he was committed to a life spent fly fishing and teaching anglers. Even though his first fish on the fly was on the Russian River in Alaska, Steve's home is in Montana and his fishing expertise has been honed and mastered on Montana's trout rivers. Fly fishing has always been in his blood. From a kid on the waters of Alaska to the creeks of Montana, Summerhill is not a self-proclaimed fanatic because fly fishing has been as much a part of his life as driving a car. In addition to guiding over 100 days a year, Steve's shop is a benchmark store for many shops throughout the United States.

*Do you feel like a lot of people misunderstand nymphing or nymph fishing?*

I do. When people think of fly fishing, they automatically picture dry-fly fishing. Dry-fly fishing is sort of the essence of fly fishing. Nymphing is the necessary part of fishing. If you are going to be successful at fly fishing, you will need to nymph. You have so many people who love dry-fly fishing, but nymphing in itself has so many nuances that are technical and difficult. The main reason why people don't give nymphing enough credit is they cannot see what is going on.

*Then is nymph fishing much more technical than most people think?*

Yes. First, the reason that it is is because most trout do most of their eating below the surface. Second, you cast your fly and you have no idea what is going on under the surface. To the average person you can't actively see what is going on. In order to be successful there are lots of things that have to be right.

*Why do you think it can be so effective?*

Simply because fish eat below the surface most of the time. People will go fishing and not catch anything, well, that's because there was not a hatch. With nymphing fish are always feeding at some point or another.

*What are some basic principles that people new to nymphing will need to know before they even get to fishing?*

When you talk about just the act of catching, nymphing is the "down-and-dirty-bare-bones way to catch a fish." Those fish are hanging out on the bottom of the river, and a nymph that floats by is easy to eat. They have to exert the least amount of energy. If you are fishing the right fly, it looks like most of the food that is down on the bottom. To introduce someone to nymphing you talk about the fish that are on the bottom, your fly has to be on the bottom, and you have to see that they are eating the fly. Seeing that eat or strike is often misunderstood.

*What about the rod? Does that factor into anyone's decision to nymph?*

I think the rod is important. In order to accomplish some basic things while nymphing, such as casting split shot on your leader, one or two weighted flies, and an indicator, you have to have a rod that can get it done. A heavier five-weight or six-weight and some instances a seven-weight. As far as fishing with an indicator, you probably won't notice more strikes because you have a certain type of rod. A heavier rod may help with casting, but not with detecting a strike. And say you are fishing without an indicator and you are swinging soft hackles; a rod that has a softer tip is really important.

*What about fly lines?*

Most fly lines nowadays will work fine. Most weight-forward fly lines are designed with a progressive front taper. They are designed to get people who really don't know how to cast—how to cast! Or to get them to cast better! The current lines will cast heavier things better. The guides these days really like the new lines because they all tend to be weighted heavier in the front of the line.

*So, if you are an angler who wants to get into nymphing, you don't need to specialize your line?*

I don't think so.

*What about any other gear that you might suggest?*

The biggest push and craze is for fluorocarbon. On certain rivers, say the Missouri, fluorocarbon is almost necessary. Fluorocarbon inherently wants to sink, so it gets your fly down faster. Secondly, you can fish a heavier fluorocarbon. For example you can fish a 6X fluorocarbon instead of 5X monofilament. And there is the thought that fluorocarbon is invisible once in the water.

*We've covered a lot of the basics, so now you have an angler who has never nymphed before, how might you explain what is going to happen? We are geared up and ready to hit the water.*

The biggest thing is to assume that we are fishing with a strike indicator. For most trout fishing an indicator is important. I would tell them to fish that indicator much like you would if it were a dry fly. You want that dead or drag-free drift so your indicator floats natural. I use the analogy of what does a stick or a piece of foam look like floating down the river. You want your indicator to do that as well—drifting naturally in the water.

*How important is getting that drag-free drift?*

Generally speaking it is very important. When fish become selective, a dead or drag-free drift makes all the difference in the world. Now, having said that, one thing that I notice on certain rivers there is a certain amount of drag that can be a good thing. It is hard to explain, but you can see it when someone is on a guided trip fishing from a boat and is drifting nymphs and is getting a little drag; they may catch more than a guide who is fishing from a boat and getting perfect dead drifts. It just shows that there are some instances where a little drag may help. A lot of times fish will key on movement, and with certain flies it is a good thing.

*What about indicators? There are nearly 100 types of indicators out there to use.*

This is purely from a guiding standpoint, meaning what is the easiest for most folks to use, and what is readily available. I like the cork balls. They are a lighter cork, but they float on everything. With that said, there are a lot of different techniques for all the various types of water one can fish. For example, on a tailwater or spring creek, I would probably not take a big cork ball and plunk it on a spring creek. For day in and day out I like the cork ball indicators.

*What about split shot?*

Dealing with split shot was one of the biggest I had to learn. I don't like to use weight if I don't have to. Usually I start a day off with no weight and go from there. If we're not catching fish, then it might be time to add weight. And vice versa, if we know we are in the fish, then it might be time to take off weight or change flies.

*Would you typically fish a fly that has weight in or add weight to the leader?*

Two sides to that. Woolly Buggers and streamers I like to have a little weight tied into the fly. With that being said not too much weight already in the fly because it is very easy to add weight, but it is very hard to take off weight that is tied into the fly. For example, on the lower Madison west of Bozeman, the river isn't very deep so too much weight will cause problems. There are some tungsten beads that are great for smaller flies. Bead-head flies are great because that gets the fly down that much faster.

*Do you have a general rule about how far from the fly you add the weight?*

If it is a Woolly Bugger, I will add it close to the fly, about 2 inches. If it is a nymph, it will be about 8–10 inches. I don't like to add it too far away because my goal is to get the fly down. If you put it too far, it is not as effective.

*Would you say that good nypmhers need a lot of imagination and optimism?*

I would say that you've got to be where the fish are. Reading the water is the basis of success. You've got to have the ability to get the fly to float with a dead drift. When that doesn't work you have to have the ability to move your fly to where it needs to be in a given run or pocket or seam so that the position of the fly may entice a strike.

*How do you get people to understand what is going on under the strike indicator?*

For the most part people don't understand what is going on under the strike indicator. A lot of people think that the fly is right under the indicator while your drift is happening. To be a good nympher you must grasp the technical part of nymphing of when to put a mend in it or just how deep the flies need to be. A lot of that just comes with getting out there and doing it. Once you can consistently put the fly in the right spot, then you can begin to think about what is going on under that indicator.

*How do you know when to set the hook?*

I set the hook on any sort of movement of that indicator. I always tell people if you see it twitch just a bit, set the hook. People miss a ton of fish. When I came to Montana I had to adjust. In Alaska everything was by feel. Here I thought I could do that as well. I'd catch a couple here and there, but my friend was catching double of what I was, so I put one on and was blown away by how many strikes I had been missing. Good fishermen will set the hook before the indicator even moves. It might be one of those sixth-sense things, but if you put the cast right, your indicator is in the right spot, and then it barely moves and it is a strike. For a beginning nympher I tell them don't be afraid to set the hook on anything.

*How hard do you think people need to set the hook?*

I like to teach the tip-set. Just move the rod tip just a bit. That way you don't have to cast again if it is not a hit. If there is nothing there, meaning it is not a fish, then you can throw a mend in the line and continue fishing. If there is something there, then you set it with vigor. The most common thing with beginners is they are fishing with too much slack to begin with that the tight line never gets to the fish. The second issue they set so hard they are probably pulling it out of the fish. Lastly, people need to set the hook straight up and down. A lot of people set the hook side-arm, and that can pull the fly right out of the fish's mouth.

### What are some problems that you see in experienced anglers?

The way people set the hook. Often times I see experienced anglers fishing with the line in the left hand and the rod in the right hand. This is normal fishing, but with nymphing when they set the hook they haul on the line with the left hand while pulling with the rod in their right hand; they are in essence just putting a single haul in the fly line. People pull the fly out of the fish's mouth by doing this. If they simply pinch the line against the rod with the index finger of their right hand, that will hook those fish. The line is coming tight rather than being pulled in a direction. Lock that line under your index finger of your rod hand and set straight up!

### What about any casting adjustments?

You need to open up your casting loop. With nymph rigs you need to cast a sloppier, wider loop.

### What about leader adjustments? Length? Diameter size?

Depending on the water you are fishing, you need to adjust. For tailwaters like the Missouri, Bighorn, Beaverhead, you need to lengthen the leader and decrease its diameter. That allows for better drift and action of those smaller flies.

### What about depth of the indicator?

I like to have my indicator as close to my fly as possible. If I am fishing shallow water and I have my indicator 7 feet from my fly, a fish could eat the fly, salt and pepper the thing, put it on the barbecue, and then spit it out before I even know what is going on! As a general rule, I start with my indicator roughly 5 feet from the fly. If fishing deeper water, the indicator moves up so the fly is fishing deeper, shallow water the indicator moves down so it is fishing less deep. One thing is that people assume that even in deeper water the fish are on the bottom, and that is not always the case.

*Would you agree that once you can get someone to actively think about what their fly is doing under the water and then adjust their technique with mends, strips, and raising or lowering the rod, they will catch a lot more fish?*

Yes. I agree completely. Once you start to realize what is going on under the water, your skill level and success level goes up dramatically. Related to that is making sure you are focused on the big picture— looking at the surface and speed of the water, the depth, and what your fly line is doing. Don't be so focused on just the indicator. Once you can ease your focus from the indicator, then some of the other things may be more clear and then you may see more things happen.

*Give me your top three nymphs in the following situations:*

*General fishing situation or searching a new piece of water:* Prince Nymph, Hare's Ear, and Pheasant Tail. Go back to basics.

*Expecting a hatch of mayflies:* Pheasant Tail, Hare's Ear, and any soft hackle pattern.

*Caddis:* Prince Nymph, Hare's Ear, any soft hackle pattern but skittered and stripped.

*Stoneflies:* Prince Nymph, dead-drifted Woolly Buggers, and Girdle Bug or Yuk Bug.

*You mentioned soft hackles. How might anglers fish soft hackles?*

They are great flies because you can dead-drift them and they have their own action in them. Or you can drag or lift them through the water and they imitate an emerging insect. Using soft hackles goes back to that imagination aspect of nymphing. You've got to be willing to try a few things to see what works.

*Do you think most anglers nymph out of fun or out of necessity?*

I think it is mixed. Of course dry-fly fishing is the most fun and most visual. However, nymphing can be so effective that it can be just as much fun nymphing as it can be casting to rising fish.

**Quick-Glance Summary:**

Nymphing is necessary

Fish eat under the surface most of the time

Weight-forward fly line

Dead or drag-free drift is key

Tinker with your rig, be flexible

Reading water is the basis of nymphing

Anticipate the strike

Set on any movement

Set with the rod tip

Cast a wider loop

# Getting the Goods

## Gearing Up, Rigging Up, or Gearing Down

### What is the one rod I should own? For trout? For saltwater?

In the 1990s, for half a decade, I owned just one fly rod: a 9-foot, five-weight Sage. It was stiff enough to cast streamers with, long enough to nymph with, stiff enough to cast a hopper into the wind, and possessed just enough subtlety to make reasonable presentations with small flies. I practically slept with that rod. It wasn't a top-shelf Sage, but it got the job done and then some, and had what I now think of as "good ju-ju."

These days there are literally a dozen rod companies that make great all-around trout rods and a dozen more that make serviceable versions. Echo makes the best inexpensive good trout rod I know of, and it retails for around $150. A Winston BIIIx and Sage One are impeccable rods, but they retail for somewhere around seven-bills. Are they better rods than the Echo? Absolutely. Are they four times better? That depends on how nuanced the angler's sensibility is.

So, what is the single rod I should own for trout? If I lived in the Midwest and fished brushier streams, I might go with an 8½-foot five-weight as my all-a-rounder, but since I mostly fish big Western rivers, a 9-foot rod is my choice—the extra 6 inches go a long way to aid in mending, punching flies through the wind, and setting the hook at distance. A six-weight in the same length wouldn't be a bad decision, but it would make delicate casts to sippers very difficult.

If I could only own one rod for the salt, I would choose a 9-foot eight-weight rod; anything lighter and I'd often find myself a bit under-gunned in the standard 20-mile-per-hour gusts one encounters on the flats, and plum worthless when the wind really started to blow. An eight-weight is perfect for redfish, bonefish, baby tarpon, seatrout, snapper, snook, and stripers, and in a pinch will work for permit (though lead-eyed crab flies are easier to cast with a nine-weight). Here it is worth noting that while I would be happy fishing with a middle-of-the-road five-weight trout rod most of the time, I do not feel the same way about saltwater gear. Success is so much the rarer in saltwater fly fishing that one really wants to be prepared to the nines, with the absolute top-flight gear.

### What is a double-taper fly line? Why might I want it?

Of course, a rod, even the world's best, is worthless without a fly line. In fresh water, in most situations, I use a floating line, either a weight-forward (WF) or a double-taper (DT). Some rods "load" or flex better if you "over-line" them one weight—that is, often times a stiff five-weight casts better with a 6-weight line, but these are special situations. In general, you want to line your rod according to its weight, and choose one of the aforementioned options. In general, a weight-forward line casts better in short-range situations, while a double-taper has an economic advantage: When it becomes dirty and cracked, it can be reversed, tied to the backing again, and the fresh "end" can be fished for several months.

One last note about cleaning fly lines: You'll never be disappointed if you clean your fly line daily, but you might be if you don't. Whether wade-fishing or drift-fishing, you'll inevitably step on your fly line, abrading it and pushing dirt into these abrasions. These cracks and dirt cause the floating line to sink, which puts unnecessary drag on the fly. Sometimes just a hint of drag on the fly will turn a fish away from the bug. Like every sport, fly fishing is often a game of minutia. Thus, cleaning fly lines is both economically and piscatorially sound.

## Is there an advantage to fluorocarbon tippet and leaders?

Since I began fishing hard in the early 1990s, a debate has stewed among anglers as to whether fluorocarbon tippet is superior to monofilament. It is certainly more expensive. A 30-yard spool of 5X fluoro, for instance, will cost you $15, while a 120-yard spool of mono will cost about the same. Invented in 1972 in Japan and released to the United States roughly two decades ago, fluorocarbon was touted as more abrasion-resistant, faster-sinking, and less visible than monofilament. For these reasons, it quickly became the favored tippet material of nymph fishermen, but many anglers balked at the cost and were deterred by the fact that it is far less biodegradable than normal nylon (monofilament) tippet material.

As strong as it is, fluorocarbon's price is often, ultimately, a deterrent for some anglers. And I know many great fly fishers who simply do without it. Many critics point to the fact that many brands of fluorocarbon "cut themselves" when a wind knot finds its way into the line—so check your tippet often for nicks and knots.

Personally, when rigging for deep nymphing, I like to use a fluorocarbon leader, or at least a long chunk of quick-to-sink tippet. I also won't be caught without it when fishing small dry flies on a spring creek or on a river with slick braided currents such as the lower Clark Fork.

## Do I need a large arbor reel?

Like fluorocarbon, another piece of nice but ultimately unnecessary gear is the large arbor reel. Because of their increased arbor size, these reels can hold more backing and retrieve line more quickly than a standard arbor reel. Again, these reels are nice but wholly a luxury. As many great trout anglers have said, including the late great Tom

Harman, reels are merely "glorified line holders." We younger anglers feel reels are "man bling" . . . exciting to own and fish and will generate some oohs and ahhs, but our predecessors pretty much got it right.

### What is all this talk about rod action?

In terms of equipment, what matters most is the rod in the angler's hands. Each rod one holds will have a different "feel" to it, an individual flexibility and stiffness. When I was breaking into the sport, you could generalize about a rod company's reputation—Sages are stiff as boards, we used to say, while Winstons are limp as noodles—but these days companies build so many models of rods as to render generalizations useless. Sage now makes extremely stiff rods, like the TCX their new very flexible and soft Circa; and Winston's Boron IIIx is the antithesis of the supple, old-school IM6.

This is all to say that you must find the rod that feels right for you. Nowadays, fly rods are a lot like California Pinot Noirs—there's a lot of nuance if you've got the palate to distinguish, and even if you don't, it's hard to go wrong.

# Expert Advice: Drew Miller

## Double the Pleasure:
## Tandem Rigs

*Grizzly Hackle*
Missoula, Montana
www.grizzlyhackle.com

Born and raised in the Laurel Mountains of southwestern Pennsylvania, Drew Miller grew up fishing small, sometimes unnamed freestone streams. After completing an undergrad degree at Indiana University of Pennsylvania in secondary education, Miller packed up his gear and moved to Montana with the intention of becoming a guide. In July of 1997 in Missoula, the last stop on his "find-work-now" trek across the state, Miller landed a job working behind the counter at the famed Grizzly Hackle Fly Shop and began guiding wade-trips (or as longtime guides called them, "boot jobs") on Rock Creek that fall. Soon, riding the *A River Runs Through It*–induced spike in area business, Miller was guiding full time and quickly became one of the most respected young oarsmen on the Clark Fork, Bitterroot, and Blackfoot Rivers. Like all great guides, Miller—now the Grizzly Hackle's Orvis-endorsed head guide and full-time outfitter—"fishes through (his) clients" and knows the fine line between providing pertinent fishing information and overloading his clients with instruction. In addition to guiding upwards of 140 days a year, he designs fly patterns for Montana Fly Company and fishes worldwide.

*When you first arrived in Missoula and after the euphoria began to wear off, what was the first thing you noticed about Western rivers in respect to the streams you grew up fishing?*

What I immediately noticed was the amount of fish that were available to the average angler, and then very quickly the vast amount of water, the endless miles of rivers and small streams. I knew it was more water than I could ever cover. If you thought about it too much, it could seem overwhelming.

*How about the size of the rivers, did that seem overwhelming?*

That wasn't too intimidating because I was lucky enough to get into a drift boat early on. Fishing from a boat can make a river seem smaller because you're seeing the water from the inside out. And in drift boat fishing, the tandem rig is something everybody out West uses because you can cover so many feeding zones; I was introduced early to dropper techniques, and they helped me break the big rivers down.

*You arrived out West during what some might call the "dawn of dropper fishing."*

Yeah, the magazines had just started talking about it, and bead-heads were everywhere. It was hard to find a nymph without a bead on it. In contrast, when I was down in Chile in 2004, I showed my veteran Chilean guide a hopper-dropper rig. He held up his finger and said, "You know, that might work!"

*Anglers have been fishing multiple fly rigs for centuries—the old-time soft-hackle fishermen sometimes using three flies—but was there someone out West who first converted you to this style of fishing and guiding?*

My first year as a full-time guide, I was guiding with an older outfitter from Deer Lodge named Pat Bannon on the Blackfoot River in August. The standard tactic back then was to fish a big hair-wing dry down the middle of the river, and that's what I was doing, without too much success. Behind me, though, Pat had his clients sticking fish left and right. I eddied out and let him catch up to me so that I could ask him what he was using. He didn't mind showing me his rig: a Schroeder's parachute hopper with a 3-foot dropper and a small split shot above a big hare's ear nymph—I don't know why he wasn't using a bead-head; maybe he didn't believe in them. But that was the turning point for me. I saw how deadly the technique could be because it made marginal days good days.

*Okay, let's say you're speaking to an angling neophyte who has just arrived for his first fishing trip; explain to this angler why dropper fishing can be more productive than fishing with a single dry.*

Well, anytime I find myself in a non-hatch situation—okay, 90 percent of the time I find myself in a non-hatch situation—I'm going to have my clients fishing some kind of tandem rig. Number one, you're showing the fish two food sources in two different feeding lanes, not to mention that as most people know, the majority of a trout's food is found beneath the water's surface. It's a sure way to dramatically increase your odds in hooking up with fish, especially highly pressured fish, to boot.

*Technically speaking, what are some specific examples of tandem rigs you use with clients, and can you take us through the how and why of each?*

Sure. Let's start with the double-dry fly rig, which is one I find myself going to more often than not, especially when I'm in a situation where dual hatches are going on. In the spring on Missoula's rivers, this double-dry rig might be a skwala stonefly trailed by a gray drake imitation; in the fall, I might use a parachute mahogany trailed by a smaller, less visible baetis. Or sometimes I'll use the double-dry to cover two stages of the same hatch, like the dun-spinner rig during the Trico hatch/fall when individual fish are keying on different stages of insect. There are lots of days around here when the snooty fish on the Clark Fork and lower Bitterroot will discern between a female Trico and a male, with each different fish preferring a differ-ent fly. The double-dry rig, with the bugs about 16 to 22 inches apart, is about the only way to sort that problem out.

You can also use the double-dry rig to prospect with when there are no hatch bugs available at all. You know, a hopper-ant combo works well in late summer when terrestrials are out and about. A Stimulator-Royal Wulff combo is a great one in fast pocket water.

As for different ways to use dropper rigs, people generally think of the hopper-dropper as being the extent of tandem rigs, but my favorite dropper technique is actually to take a *very visible* but small parachute fly, say a #16 Parachute Adams, and tie a tiny bead head like a pheasant tail or an RS2 2 inches beneath the dry fly. This tech-nique is deadly on real picky tailwater fish, especially during a dense hatch. It's not dry-fly fishing per se, because the fish are more often than not eating the sunken fly, but it's a great way to fish because you will still see the fish take your fly. This technique works well on the Missouri and the Clark Fork when the sheer number of naturals is what's keeping your fly from being eaten, and is a real day-saver on spring creeks.

### Why is visibility so important with the dry fly?

You've got to have a fly that you can see, because you've got to be able to react to the fly disappearing. If you can't see it, it can't disap-pear. So start with a good floater like a Royal Wulff, something with a fluffy silhouette. I'll use this in a situation such as fishing sunken spinners. I use that "Sink" made by the makers of "Gink" to get the small dropper fly down. When you have a big pod of fish rising and you're trying to get someone to pick your fly out of the millions on the surface, there's always an opportunistic fish that has been pushed out of the frenzy and is willing to take something else.

*How about dropping nymphs beneath your dries?*

Here, the length of the dropper tippet makes a huge difference, but generally I go with a pretty deep—3 to 4 feet—dropper. Most people don't realize that you can get away with fishing a 4-foot dropper in shallow water, but you can. If you use a lightly weighted nymph, it will get kicked up from the bottom just like a natural and will move like a natural, too.

Then there are cases when I'm fishing a deep hole, say 10 feet, but I don't want too deep of a dropper because the fish are suspended 18 inches beneath the surface eating emerging nymphs or drowned duns. Then maybe the next day, in that same hole, the fish are back on the bottom and I have to fine-tune my techniques.

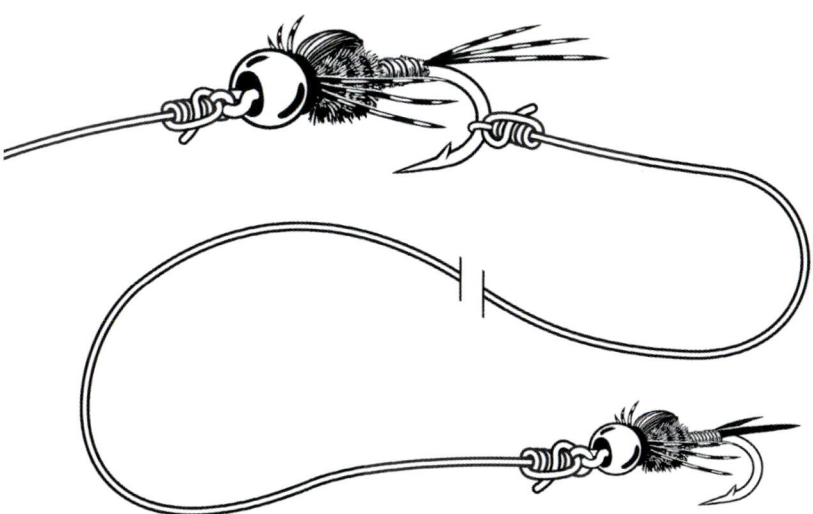

### Two-Fly Hook Bend

Two-fly rig with trailer hook tied off the bend of the hook.

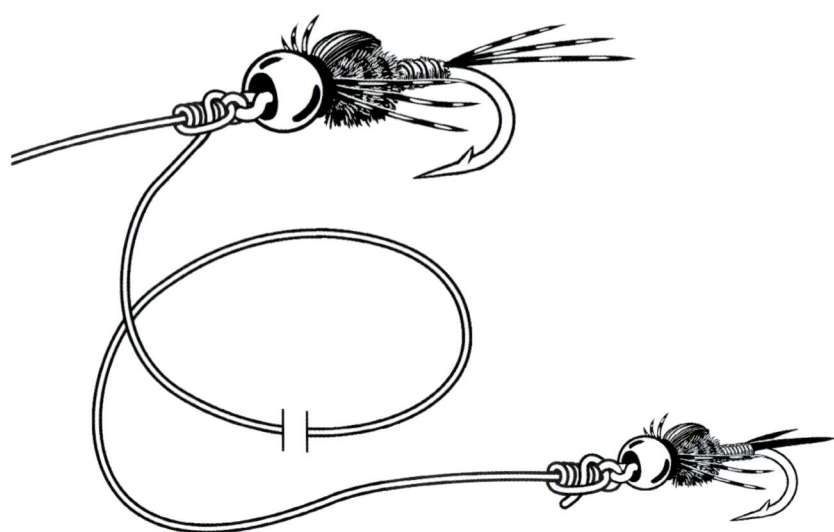

### Two-Fly Knot Tag Trailer

Two-fly rig with trailer hook tied from an intentional, extremely long tag end left from the tying of the top fly.

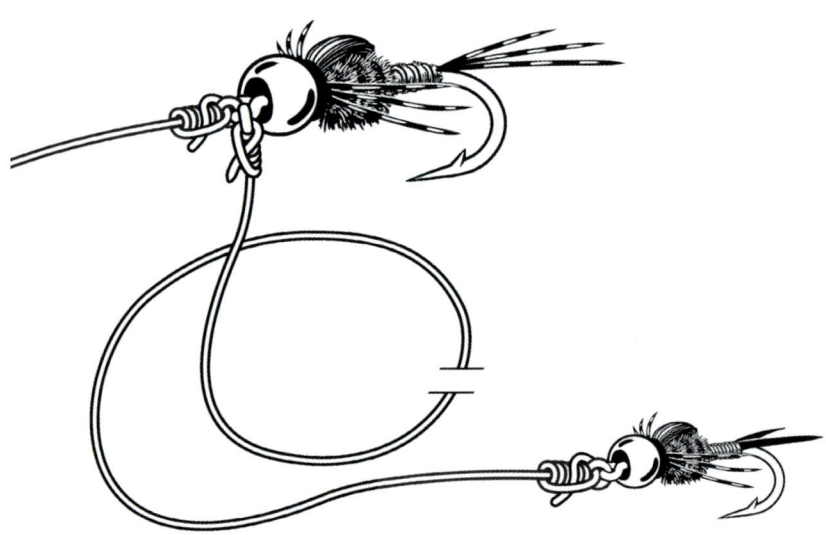

### Two-Fly Two Knot Trailer

Two-fly rig with trailer hook tied with a separate clinch knot tied onto the eye of the fly.

*How so?*

Well, if I were to give a piece of simple advice to someone fishing a new river, it would be "adjust your dropper often." Begin with a general pattern, like a prince or a pheasant tail, something that works everywhere out West, and vary your dropper length to the water type. Also, vary the weight of your dropper. This might seem insignificant, but I'll carry, say, bead-head Prince Nymphs in size 12-18, and then carry the exact same flies with tungsten beads. What I've found is that the tungsten bead on a short, 1-foot dropper has an important role in fast shallow water. Basically, I learned this by experimenting when my go-to tactics failed; I wasn't catching fish on deep droppers where I knew fish were, so I started playing around with things. It's all about adjusting weight and distance; you just have to dial each river in each day.

*This might seem like a silly question, but how do you know when a fish takes your nymph dropper?*

There's no way to know. You always assume it's a fish. Your guide has most likely trained his eyes to see the slightest twitch or tilt on the indicator fly, so another way of "knowing" is just to set the hook when he says to! There are times when I've been on the water for two weeks straight and I'll just see the indicator fly pause, and tell my client to set, and sure enough the fish will be there, despite the client's doubts. You just cannot be fast enough. I've watched fish eat and spit out a bead head or emerger 2 inches beneath the indicator fly, and not move the dry fly an inch.

*Do you find that your clients foul-hook a lot of fish with droppers?*

I see it happen fairly often, and I don't know how to prevent it. A lot of times, the fish will come up to grab the dry fly, you'll miss him, and the dropper will catch him right on the outside corner of the mouth. The worst place to foul-hook a fish is of course in the tail, because a fighting fish can't get any oxygen that way. When that happens, I just tell my clients to strip 'em in.

*Beginners can find fishing with two flies difficult. What sort of instruction do you give your green clients to keep them from tangling their rigs all day?*

What I generally do with beginners is start them out with a heavy shorter leader, like a 7-foot, tapered to 2X. This leader allows the beginner to turn the flies over. And even if the cast looks sloppy—I'll still give them a 4-foot dropper—the cast can still catch fish: there's a difference between a perfect cast and a fishing cast.

I also try to make sure that they stop the rod on the backcast at twelve o'clock sharp. I call it the Wyatt Earp cast—just stop it high and gun it out there.

Another place beginners have to be careful is on the hook set. A lot of times they'll just ease it out of the water. Make the whole rig come all the way out of the water. When you set, come up swinging, hard enough that your line straightens out behind you, and you can re-cast.

*Do you ever come across a client, a purist of sorts that simply refuses to fish a tandem rig? What do you say to this type of angler?*

I'll usually tell them, "It's your trip, so you can fish however you like." I use droppers because they're effective, not because they're necessary. But most days I usually have two clients in the boat, and if one of them is a "purist," the other one is there to catch fish. Usually when I see this situation, I think, my day is made, because the purist will be converted by about lunchtime.

And I'm not using a tandem rig all day. I usually have three rods rigged for each client—a dry-fly rig, a hopper-dropper rig, and an indicator nymph rig. And we'll fish those rigs as conditions demand, fishing the dry fly in the slick water to risers, and the nymph rig when we get to the heavy pockets. It's just like golfing: "Give me the 9-iron for this shot."

*Are there any situations in which you won't fish a two-fly rig?*

Sure, because fishing a dropper is definitely more difficult for every-one; even good casters have to learn to open up their loop to allow for the hinge the dropper creates in the cast. Sometimes if it's really windy, I'll just have a client nymph with an indicator and split shot because the weight of the rig carries it through the wind more easily. I'll also cut the dropper off when it's necessary to cast really tight to bank-cover, although a good, downstream-angled cast will let you fish a dry and a dropper tight to logs and undercut banks. There are also days, often when fish are taking small flies on the surface, that a drop-per puts just enough micro-drag on the dry that trout avoid it in spots they would otherwise take it. And I've had moments where it seems that the ever-attractive gold bead is more of a detractor, and fish prefer a more subtle copper bead, or no bead on the dropper fly at all, maybe just a small split shot above the nymph.

*Do you ever see instances where the dropper tippet gets in the way of clients hooking fish?*

You know, I don't have any conclusive evidence on this one way or the other. Some days it seems like this is the case, but I think fish eat dif-ferently on different days. One day they might be hammering the dry fly and almost hooking themselves, and the next day they might be mouthing or pushing the fly, being real careful. I do think it's impor-tant, especially with foam flies, to check often that your leader is not wrapped around the hook bend or the eye of the hook, because that will absolutely alter your effectiveness in hooking fish.

*What are, to you, some dropper fishing absolutes?*

When I'm fishing the hopper-dropper rig, the first thing I look for is a foam or parachute hair-wing fly that lands upright and floats all day. You don't want a fly to start sinking just when it's getting into the strike zone. The next thing I do is make sure I'm cycling through my standards—princes, pheasant tail, hare's ear variations, San Juan worm—with different dropper depths until I find the right setup. Keep experimenting. That's what makes fly fishing so interesting and fun. If it wasn't a complex game, we wouldn't enjoy it so much. It's a puzzle, and you have to put the pieces together every day.

*After guiding roughly 1,000 days on Montana's rivers, do you feel like you're still learning about them and the trout that live within them?*

Absolutely. One of the nice things about being an Orvis-endorsed guide is that we get written feedback from the clients via Orvis. A lot of pressure gets put on guides to catch fish, to get it done, but even a good guide can't control everything. I've learned to be someone who guides hard when he needs to. There are situations where you have to instruct on every cast and every drift; and then there are times when you have to just allow people to fish and digest what they are doing.

## Quick-Glance Summary:

Different foods in different feeding lanes

Double dry, or dry and dropper

Highly visible, good floating dry fly

Droppers can be 2 inches to 4 feet

Adjust dropper length and weight to find the best combination

Cast like Wyatt Earp

Strike hard and fast

# Uber-Techy Fly Fishing

## Spring Creeks and
## Small Dry-Fly Situations

Ahhh, spring creeks: intimate, often hidden bodies of water that offer clear water of a consistent temperature nearly 365 days a year, not to mention big trout that feed consistently and discriminately on small to microscopic bugs. Most anglers, particularly experienced ones, have frequent, often wet, dreams about fishing spring creeks, and for very good reason.

### What is considered a spring creek?

Any body of water that is fed consistently from an underground source can safely be considered a spring creek. Some spring creeks head underground, or under water, and some pour right out of cliffs; some are boiling hot and attract soakers, and some stay cold all year and hold big trout consistently. Flow in a spring creek is usually uniform and fairly moderate, though it's worth noting here that spring ponds or spring-fed back channels, especially when adjacent to rivers, often hold big trout too.

### Why do they have such a reputation for being so technical?

Since they're clear as a wineglass polished by your grandma, flow relatively slowly but with multiple conflicting surface currents, and contain an abundance of food, spring creeks are rightly considered the home of technical fishing. What's more, the trout that live in spring creeks feed chiefly on food items that are very small and require exact imitation. For instance, even a big Trico-sipping trout on the main stem of the Bitterroot, which is considered a fairly technical river in its lower reaches, can feed like a sailor on furlough compared to its cousin in the shallow, slow-flowing spring-fed backchannel nearby.

On spring creeks, the ante is upped. To succeed here you'll need longer, lighter leaders—start at 12 and be ready to go to 17 feet—and an absolutely keen imitation of what's on the water to fool these fish, because in the clear slow flow, they get a longer, more precise look at the fly. Of course, in addition to trying to cast a leader almost twice as long as you're accustomed to casting, you'll also be trying to bury a hook that's usually four sizes smaller—think 22s and 24s—than you're used to. On top of that, your fly will be lashed to tippet that tests as light as 2⅓ pounds, and you'll be trying to land a fish that's twice that weight, while steering the trout through weeds and cress and under-cuts choked with roots and logs.

## What is the one biggest adjustment to make when fishing a spring creek?

Growing up near Bozeman with its proximity to BenHart and Thompson's Spring Creek, as well as Livingston's storied DePuy's and Nelson's, I spent a lot of time getting my proverbial butt handed to me by spring creek fish. As a young angler, I could catch plenty of fish on big rivers like the Madison, and smaller waters like the East Gallatin, but when I'd head to the spring creeks, I'd come away shaking my head.

Why wouldn't those fish take my size 12 Prince Nymph, I wondered. It works everywhere else. Occasionally, late in the day, I would get a fish to jump mercifully on a Woolly Bugger, but for the most part I struck out.

What I didn't realize, what nobody told me, was that everything matters just a little bit more on a spring creek. This means that when you're walking up to a spring creek, walk more slowly, with more stealth, than you would if you were on your way to nymph a heavy riffle on the Gallatin. Trade that white t-shirt for a long-sleeve camouflaged print, and, most importantly, sit and wait and watch awhile before casting your fly.

Ultra-technical fishing on a spring creek is a lot like fishing the flats for bonefish: If you don't see a fish, don't cast.

## Can you nymph-fish a spring creek?

Sure, you can do some blind fishing on spring creeks with small streamers, terrestrials, and the like. Years ago I had an old client who used to clean up on DePuy's spring creek with an attractor called the H&L Variant in smaller sizes, just after the PMD hatch waned.

As for nymphing, there are two ways to do it on a spring creek. The first is the very challenging but rewarding "sight-nymphing," and the second is "blind nymphing" the conventional way, with an indicator rig.

A good sight nymph-fisherman is about as rare as a three-dollar bill. Because it requires patience, incredibly keen eyesight, and deft hand-eye coordination, sight-nymphing takes great patience and skill. Some of the best nymph fishermen I know grew up steelheading in the Midwest, and learned early how to distinguish fishy forms near the bottom of the stream from logs and rocks. Hint: Look for the moving shadows of things on the stream-bottom, and keep your eyes peeled for white: this equals open mouth, usually, or belly. When sight-nymphing in shallow water, a small dry fly can often serve as an indicator, but often the indicator won't move before the fish has taken and spit the hook. You have to become attuned to fish behavior and movements. If a fish moves, or you see the white of the mouth, and your fly is in the wheelhouse, set the hook—there's a 50/50 chance you were right.

Even when nymphing with an indicator on spring creeks, the takes can be subtle. Remember, these fish have an abundance of food at their disposal, and most of the food they eat is small. A 20-inch rainbow isn't generally going to go gangbusters to eat its hundredth scud of the day. So, if your indicator even quivers, set the hook.

When looking for water to nymph "blind" on spring creeks, look for depth and chop. A 3-foot-deep riffle on a spring creek can hold some astoundingly big fish. Cutbanks, prevalent on grassy meadow streams, are also a good place to start as they offer shade and a constant stream of terrestrials (yes, ants do sink). A good combo to start with is some scud or sowbug imitation coupled with a general nymph such as a pheasant tail. I've always been partial to the unbeaded, traditional Sawyer's Pheasant Tail that my friend Alex Lafkas, an outstanding guide on Michigan's AuSable, turned me on to years ago.

### What's all this talk about "head hunting" for rising trout?

"Head hunting" is a term reserved for those who like to cast only for fish they've seen rise, sippers, as they're often called. Though I'm not one of them, there are plenty of head-hunting snobs out there, and they spend a lot of time on spring creeks, or giant spring creeks, as tailwaters are often called. Watching sippers go to work on spring creeks can be especially rewarding, since these fish are some of the wariest in running water. I like nothing more than watching a big trout get into an unabashed feeding rhythm, get super comfortable with real bugs, before I put a fake one right down his food line.

### What are some tricks to use for seeing a small dry fly?

While spotting small dry flies can be tough, the more you fish, the better your eyesight will become. There are dozens of fly patterns out there that are tied to be exceedingly visible, but frankly some of the best spring creek patterns are just tiny, low profile, and plum hard to see. True, you can fish a bigger indicator fly, like an ant or Royal Wulff, a few inches in front of your tough-to-see emerger or floating nymph, but this two-fly combo often screws up your drift.

It's better to learn to see the little "invisible" stuff that the fish really want to eat. How does one do this? First off, learn to cast a straight line.

Many anglers have trouble spotting their fly on the water because they throw a tailing loop and have no idea where their fly has landed. Once you know where your fly has landed, you can track it all the more easily through the glare and tricky currents. Next, get low to the water. Look for the impression your fly makes on the surface of the water, and that will distinguish it from the naturals on the water. Finally, if you think a fish has taken your fly, set the hook.

### Do I set the hook really fast?

But gently! When I'm guiding on the big rivers, and a fish takes the fly, I'll often yell, "Set!" But when I'm guiding on the creeks, I always try to say, calmly, "Lift." All you have to do on a hook set with a long leader is lift the rod and tighten the line. Let the fish itself set the hook. A nice long, limber three-weight rod will help cushion the light 7X tippet, but you have to do your part too, and avoid the "Bass Pro Shops Set."

### Should I have a separate arsenal of gear?

To really fish a spring creek effectively, it helps to have a more subtle line of gear than big river fishing requires. But, truth be told, I got by fishing my 9-foot five-weight on the Paradise Valley creeks for many years. You just have to be more careful with your hook set and cast.

A three- or four-weight rod is ideal for spring creek fishing because it allows you enough strength to set the hook but not so much that you crack off every fly you tie to 7X; also, the lighter rod allows you to play fish aggressively without compromising the tippet—you'd be surprised, but even with 7X, with a three-weight rod, you can put the heat on bruiser trout and not break off fish.

### What are five things an angler can do to help their presentation?

As I've covered elsewhere in the book, "presentation" doesn't just mean casting and mending; rather, "presentation" is the whole picture, from approach to position to cast to mend to hook-set to fight. On spring creeks, it's imperative that you make your best presentation first—it's like asking a supermodel to dance: you get one, very slim chance to make it happen.

To wit, I've compiled a list of five essential things an angler can do to help improve his or her presentation on spring creeks.

- POSITION: As with any fly cast onto moving water, the fly's drift is dependent on the angle of the line and the position from where the cast came. This is a very complicated way of saying, even with a good cast and adept line management, you can't compensate for a cast that comes from the wrong angle (across too many conflicting currents) or direction (over or on top of a fish, spooking your quarry).

    When determining what's the best position from which to cast on spring creeks, many things factor into the equation. The first and most important factor is whether the cast will come directly over the head of the fish I'm targeting. On spring creeks, this straight upstream approach is usually a recipe for spooked trout. So, I try to find a way to present the fly directly downstream to the fish, so that the fly is the first thing the fish sees—not the leader, or the fly line, whizzing over its head.

    Stealthily changing position and offering your fly from multiple angles is one of the keys to success on spring creeks.

- CATCHABLE FISH: Over the years, I've learned that some rising fish exist on spring creeks only to torment the angler, and that these fish should be avoided unless a distinct madness is desired. There was a pod of big rainbows on the MZ ranch, for instance, that for one entire August eluded me. They held right out in the middle of a flat, 6 inches downstream from a log, and fed audibly on Trico spinners each morning. The first time I approached them, I knelt well downstream—contrary, I realize, to what I described above—and peeled my line from my reel. At the drag's zipping sound, the fish went down. "Really?" I thought. "The fish spooked at the sound of the line being pulled from the reel?" An angler not quite as pig-headed as myself could have ventured upstream and found some easier fish, but I got my ego involved.

- PERSISTENCE: Throughout that August, nearly every day, I tried these fish from a dozen different angles. Thank goodness I didn't have a job! As it was, the upstream log would not allow for the preferred downstream drift, so I had to either shoot straight upstream, directly across, or up and across at these spooky fish— and none of these options proved to elicit good drifts. After a week or so, though, I found that I could, if I casted over the fish's right shoulders, and landed the fly 3 inches below the log, I could feed the fly into one of the fish's open mouths. Of course, I sacrificed a hundred dollars' worth of flies to the log and to the trout's mouths before I finally landed the fish, but that fact seems neither here nor there.

- GO-TO: Of all the patterns I tried on these MZ Spring Creek fish, the fly that finally worked best was a #22 Royal Wulff, a fly that has since become my go-to dry fly on spring creeks. It really pays to have a go-to fly like this. Often, on spring creeks, there is such a density of food that fish have trouble distinguishing a perfect match from a natural. Some years ago I discovered that offering a fly that sticks out from the masses can often trigger strikes from otherwise hardheaded fish. With its white wings and body made of peacock herl, the Royal Wulff might have looked like a clump of Tricos to the fish that ate it, or perhaps an ant or beetle. The best part is, I'll never know.

- SITTING: This principle was covered earlier, but it's so important that it merits restatement: One of the best things you can do to increase your productivity on spring creeks is to sit and wait and watch. I can't tell you how many times I've sat eating lunch across from a grassy run I've just pounded with nymphs, and watched a big trout slip out from the undercut to take a bug. For most anglers, especially the Type A kind, there's nothing harder than peeling your eyes and sitting on your hands for a while, but I promise you it will pay off. What's more, you'll be sitting in one of the most pristine environs that trout fishing has to offer. What could be more beneficial than that?

# Expert Advice: Matson Rogers

## Spring Creek Specialties: Making the Difficult a Little Easier

*Anglers West Fly Fishing Outfitters*
Emigrant, Montana
www.montanaflyfishers.com

At seven years old, Matson ventured with his father on one of many routine fishing trips out of Aspen, Colorado. His father would always stop at Chuck Fothergill's Outdoor Sportsman shop to stock up on flies and, just as important, information. Matson constantly fingered, grabbed, and inspected all the gadgets, flies, and thingie-majigs that modern fly shops

contain. But before Matson could relish in his amazement any longer, his dad always remembered that they were there to get flies to *go* fishing rather than just *talk* about fishing. However, who would have thought that those ten-minute stops to buy some flies and shoot the breeze would shape a young child's path. Since then Matson has been pursuing his passion of guiding people on fly-fishing trips for the past sixteen years. Matson holds a degree in environmental economics from St. Lawrence University in Canton, New York, and is a former instructor at the Western Rivers Guide School in Jackson, Wyoming. Along with his home waters in Montana, Matson has fished throughout the Rockies, in New England, the Upper Midwest, Alaska, New Zealand, British Columbia, and Labrador.

*In this chapter we are talking about various skills to help anglers fish spring creeks. First, what is your definition of a spring creek and "spring creek fishing"?*
A creek or small river is most notably referred to as a spring creek when the immediate source of its flow is derived from an upwelling of spring water. Its entire flow may or may not be from one spring, but numerous spring water seepages along its course. Spring creeks are usually very rich in nutrients and aquatic weed growth, and spring creeks typically have prolific hatches of aquatic bugs. It's also very important to note that a true spring creek has a nearly constant water temperature at the source. Having a stable temperature window along with the aforementioned richness is one of the primary reasons why spring creeks are the incredible fisheries they are.

*Why is that so?*
It is the creek's ability to maintain cool water temperatures throughout the heat of summer and warmer than freezing temps through winter that make spring creeks very appealing to trout, and these characteristics make spring creeks year-round fisheries.

*There is a certain preconception that spring creeks are the most challenging fishing there is. Do you believe that? Are there times when this isn't the case?*
No, spring creek fishing is not always the most challenging fly fishing there is. There are plenty of other situations whether fly fishing fresh water or salt that can be as difficult and even surprisingly more so than fickle spring creek situations. There are times where some spring creek fishing can be downright easy. Although that's not very often! It's like any situation in the outdoor world where enthusiasts pursue wild creatures in that animal's own backyard. There are a lot of things that have to align perfectly in order to be a consistently successful hunter, photographer, or angler.

*So there have been times when spring creek fishing is easy?*

I have been fortunate to witness several multihour episodes of spring creek gluttony while guiding clients on the Paradise Valley spring creeks like Armstrong's and Depuy's. Whatever it was that made the hatches intensify and become supercharged, there was so much bug activity that normally skittish, ultra-selective trout completely lost their inhibitions and fed on absolutely everything passing by. And they were undisturbed by anglers standing in plain view, casting and otherwise moving about the creek without spooking these fish. During times like this, the fishing still isn't exactly easy, but in comparison to most spring creek situations, it is.

*What may make a spring creek more challenging than, say a small mountain stream?*

Spring creek fishing is more challenging than fishing a small mountain stream generally because of two things: current speed and window of opportunity. Small mountain streams are often steeply pitched and follow a course through boulders in a quick drop from pool to pool. Think about the one thing you hear when you are near a mountain stream. It's the sound of the moving water. It's fast, boisterous, churning, gurgling, and one thing is clear—it's noisy. Spend time on a spring creek and what's the one thing you don't hear? Yep, you guessed it, rushing waters. Spring creeks are best typified as a softer, more gentle course of water.

*What about the "window of opportunity" that you refer to?*

The "window" of opportunity simply refers to how long a trout has to decide to eat or not. Put the two concepts together, and you can quickly envision just how fast a trout has to make up its mind whether or not the object approaching it in the water column is food or debris in a rushing mountain stream. It's now or never. On a spring creek, the much more mellow current speed allows trout what seems to be an agonizing amount of time to inspect their food. They may be thinking, "Is it real, hmmm, let's take a really good look at it." You have to be able to have very life-like presentations in order to fool a spring creek trout.

*What are some adjustments you would make when heading out to fish a spring creek? In terms of rods and reels, leaders, fly selection, etc.*

The first thing I do is to remind myself it's time to slow down. Forget the fast pace of life, whether it's the drive to the creek or life in the office, one of the best things to do to prepare yourself for fishing on a spring creek is to take a few minutes while rigging up your gear to consciously slow down and start to observe what is going on around you. Aside from this, my spring creek equipment does tend to be a bit on the lighter, softer side of things as far as a rod goes. Same with fly line, leaders, right down to the flies I fish. One of my favorite spring creek setups is a sweet little Scott G series rod that is just the short side of a 9-footer, made for a #4 line and is characterized as a "medium" action. Don't get me wrong, it's not a noodle. Far from it. It's crisp with some real zip when it's needed, but it can lay a size 22 midge dry fly with the delicate touch of a feather floating to the water's surface on a 30-foot cast. With a fish on, the tip has just the right bend-don't-break capability that will protect my 6X tippet.

*What about leaders?*

On the terminal tackle end of things, I usually don't go to great lengths to fish anything longer that a 12-foot 5X or 6X leader. I have yet to find a commercially available leader any longer than this that will consistently turn over and give me the accuracy that I desire. One thing is for sure, however, I am a big fan of fluorocarbon leader materials. I love the stuff, and anytime I find myself nymphing, you can bet fluorocarbon is in use. I definitely believe that it has much lower visibility in the water column, which means that often times I can one up my tippet size. Example, fishing non-fluorocarbon tippet material may mean having to fish 6X tippet with small nymphs whereas I can generally get fish to eat my bugs with 5X fluoro.

*What might be the most important adjustment an angler needs to make to have success on a spring creek?*

I think one of the most important things is what I just mentioned—slowing down and observing. But to add to that, to be successful on the creeks you need to perhaps review your definition of success. Does catching ten, twenty, thirty, or more trout in a day of fishing define your success? If so, you'd best fish elsewhere. Are you capable of first becoming aware of what's going on within the microcosm of the spring creek, patiently observing the creek below its surface in order to see the fish, quietly approach the fish's lie, and determine the life cycle stage the fish may be feeding on, successfully tie on your pattern of choice to match that bug, and then make that critically important first presentation? Remember, first impressions are often the most long lasting. If this isn't something you are capable of doing, spring creek fishing might not be for you. I can't tell you how many times I get to the last step to only have the trout sense something is amiss and skedaddle on out of there before the fly even touches the surface of the water. Patience and acceptance of things you can't control, those are the most important adjustments!

*Do anglers need to be exceptional casters to have success on a spring creek?*

It certainly helps as one of the more important aspects of getting your fly in front of a spring creek trout is accuracy. That doesn't mean it has to be in a soup can from 60 feet away. How about an 8-inch pie plate at 25 feet? That's realistic. What can be just as difficult as making a 60-foot cast is actually pulling off the sneak to get within that 25-foot range. I've had numerous neophyte anglers spend a day on the spring creeks and have had solid success at getting them into their first spring creek trout. Were they exceptional casters? Far from it, but they were good students of the hunt and were able to get a decent enough cast to the target once we were able to get in as close as possible.

*Do you have any specific casts or casting adjustments that you make?*
Having the ability to fade line purposely left or right, the ability to at least start to make a respectable curve cast, a parachute cast, steeple cast, etc., are all good abilities to have. These are not necessarily as much of a prerequisite to fishing on the creeks perhaps as much as the ability to know how to properly and effectively feed and control fly line out your rod tip on a down and across presentation to a fish. If you can do this well, you can likely make up for lack of fancy casting.

*In most spring creeks there is a plethora of insect life. Do anglers need to have a complete understanding of all the bug life cycles and types of insects to catch fish?*
You don't have to have a PhD in aquatic entomology to catch fish on a spring creek. It is helpful to know your mayflies from midges, however. As long as you understand just the basic life cycle of the bugs you are looking to imitate and know where the fish are, you will find some feeding fish. There's a long-standing saying that once you've got a fly pattern that is close in resembling the size, shape, and color of the natural, it's presentation, presentation, presentation that makes for success.

*Just how important are hatches in the feeding activity of most spring creek fish?*
Hugely. What I've noticed is that there are almost always fish that can be found somewhere on a spring creek that are feeding. Even if there is a big hatch of some sort, there's still sure to be a fish or three nymphing on scuds or midge pupa or something like that. But if you want multiple targets to be able to cast to after you've either

successfully spooked the few fish you found grazing here and there, having a hatch come off almost always rings the dinner bell, and spring creek trout become a lot easier and more approachable during the hatch.

## Is time of year important?

Just to have food in the water, not necessarily. Throughout the year there are bug species available because of the consistency of water temps and rich nutrient levels. There's almost certainly going to be scuds, sowbugs, aquatic annelids, and other nymphs that will be available almost all the time, even in the winter. Certainly there is a specific time of year for each given hatch species. Each spring creek will have its own timetable. On our local creeks the general yearly timetable for hatches stays pretty much the same for the individual species. For example, saying PMDs start June 11 every year is not the case. But to say that PMDs start sometime around the second or third week of June is acceptable. If there is a specific hatch that you really want to hit, it doesn't take too much asking around with the local fly shops and guides in order to find out.

## Of all the time that you've spent fishing spring creeks, what might be some of your most difficult times and what would be some of your least difficult times? Can you elaborate as to why they were so?

Oh, man, the difficult times . . . I think one of the most difficult times is when the angler I'm guiding is all hyped up about being there, and rightfully so, and unable to calm down. If you can't sit still and relax, it can be really difficult to get into the rhythm of the creek. You need to be able to detach from everything else and simply chill out with the creek. Being ultra-focused isn't necessarily all that great either. If you get too focused, you get tunnel vision so to speak, and you may miss out on some of the little things the creek's telling you about what's going on. If there's not a hatch going on when you first get to the spot you want to fish, rushing off to the next spot and so on all up and down the creek is not what's going to make things successful. Sometimes you have to get to a spot that looks good, or you know from past experience that it is good, and you have to be willing to camp out and put in some time before moving on.

*What about some easy times?*

Some of the least difficult times have been when the creeks are really firing on all cylinders and have been for a couple of days or a week. The same cycle is apparent each day. After a bit, you know exactly when and where the fish will be, when the hatch will start up, or when it's time to move from X location to Y and just what fly patterns ought to be money. When you can set your watch by the creek's activity, that's when it's easy.

*Let's say it is early July and you are headed to one of the Paradise Valley spring creeks. What are you going to encounter? How might you approach the day?*

I'd approach the day thinking first, who's here ahead of me and where are they most likely going to be already fishing. If I see car parked in a certain area, especially if it is a car I recognize, that helps me understand if they know the creek's better fishing locations and hatch timing. If the cars are totally unfamiliar, I still have a basic game plan in my head about where I would wish to be given the time of day for the "main event" so to speak. Unless it's a spring creek that you have total access to, there's usually a little chess game that is going to take place throughout the day with the other anglers present. Knowing this and how to maneuver yourself, pawn takes knight kind of thing, can actually have a sizable impact upon your fishing.

*That's all great and good, but what about a situation where you don't have to worry about other anglers?*

Okay, throwing that aside, just the basics of what to expect in early July: it's likely that the day will be sunny and hot with an afternoon breeze kicking up around 2 or 3 p.m.. First thing to expect would be midges in the morning until about 9 a.m., when you should start to see fish moving out of the flats and into the riffles as the PMD nymphs start getting active. Around 10 or 11 you should start to see the duns emerging and the trout noticing the dries on the surface as well. PMD duns take a really long time to dry their wings before taking off, so they are like sitting ducks from the time when the nymphs are sitting in the surface film to the time the duns are fully ready to fly off. The emergence may last until 1 to 2 p.m., and then things can get real quiet for a while. It's a great time to take an afternoon nap in the shade of a big cottonwood—or go looking for some tight-lying bank-feeding brown trout that is still sucking down the very last dregs of the day's PMDs. For those that can't get enough by 5 p.m., and that cold beer isn't calling too loudly yet, there is a good chance of a spinner fall around 7 p.m. as well as some caddis activity especially the more toward dark you can stand to stay. By then it's only the truly gluttonous die-hards that are still out there or it's guides and outfitters like myself that have dropped off their exhausted companions of the day and are looking for a little R&R on the creek before tomorrow's trip.

*What about fishing a spring creek for the very first time? Some things you would do as you are heading to creek and/or getting ready to fish.*

If you can afford to do so, I'd try to walk as much of the property as you can along the creek just to get the lay of the land. Don't just jump into the very first good-looking spot without at least looking around the corner. And while you are walking look for the fish as well. Spring creek fish, if you are quiet and stay back a little from the bank's edge, are often capable of being seen from a fair distance. Find out where the fish like to stay either when resting but more importantly when feeding. Be careful when moving about so as not to spook them. On some creeks the fish will come right back within a short time, but on others, when they're gone, they're gone for a long time.

*What would be some things you would do before you even rig up a rod?*
Once I kind of know where I am going and have a basic idea of what to expect, I do one of two things. Either I head back to a given fish's location and actively try to pursue it, or I'll head back to a given pool or other location where there should be fish and then approach it as carefully as possible before starting to fish. One of the greatest things about fishing spring creeks is that I'm actively hunting a fish that has been spotted rather than fishing the general vicinity. So a lot of times I don't even have a fly actually on the rod until I have a quarry to cast to. I have to see whether I'm going to be sight-nymphing for a non-rising fish or if a dry fly will be the ticket.

*What about fly selection? What are some things anglers should consider about choosing flies for fishing a spring creek?*
One thing I've noticed with fishing on the spring creeks is that the flies that are often successful aren't always the most ornate. It's often the case that incredibly simple fly patterns that are the same size and color as the naturals are as good a place to start as anything. Flies that are too bulky or have lots of flash, jiggly-wiggly this-or-that are just not as effective. It doesn't even have to be flies that look to you and me as ultra-lifelike that work well. My motto is to keep it simple.

*Most people conjure up the quintessential picture of fly fishing when thinking of spring creeks—rising trout, long casts, and fine tippets. Is this always the case?*

Fine tippets, yes. Long casts, not if I can help it. Like I said before, I'd much prefer to spend more time getting into a better casting location, one that allows for a shorter, more accurate cast as a preferable method of fishing on a spring creek. Long casts are really cool to look at, but how many anglers can effectively see what's really going on with their fly line, leader, and fly at 50 feet or further? Your presentation from where you stand may look fine to you, but at that kind of distance, it's very difficult to manage even the most basic of microdrag on your fly and leader. And that can make a *huge* difference between a successful presentation and one that looks good from where you stand but looks like crap to the trout.

*What might be some common errors? How might anglers overcome these?*

I've said it several times over now—slow down. Take the time to sit next to the creek and observe before jumping in. Actually, don't jump. That's probably not a good idea either. Plan out your approach and try to look at all the angles before wading toward that big trout across the creek. Don't be in too big of a hurry to move onto the next likely spot, if upon first look you don't see anything immediately.

*Along with slowing down and observing, do you see angler-to-angler conflicts often?*

Hardly, as many anglers know about streamside etiquette. I'd like to think that the best way to treat other anglers you encounter when you are out is just the same as how you would like to be treated yourself. Give other anglers the courtesy of space. Don't go walking right up to them to chitchat or cut past them. Do let them know that you are aware of their presence. Do ask if it's okay to walk past them. And then give them some space. You shouldn't have to fish the very next likely location that is immediately upstream of that person. It's amazing how a little courtesy on the stream can benefit everyone.

*Is hiring a guide essential for fishing a spring creek?*

Hiring a guide is not essential; however, it can make the difference between a solid outing and getting skunked. When you do hire a guide, you're paying for their knowledge, their ability to put you in the right places at the right times, and for their ability to teach you how to become a better angler. You are effectively jump-starting the learning curve. One day with a guide could be compared to a week's worth of experiential learning on your own. And if you've never been to the location before, having a guide is money and time well spent. I have been guiding for seventeen years, and you can be assured that when I travel to a totally unknown territory and there are guides available, you know that I'm hiring one for me to be able to have a better experience.

*Would you ever discourage anyone from fishing a spring creek?*

I don't think I would necessarily discourage anyone from fishing a spring creek. But I'd like to know a little more about what that angler may have in fishing experience prior to either taking them as a guest or in recommending going to a spring creek. I've stated before you don't have to be an advanced fly fisher to be successful on a spring creek, but at the same time, I don't think I would want the very first day ever attempting to fly fish be on a spring creek unless it's quite clear that the expectation level for successfully catching and landing a fish is not the primary focus.

*And the flip-side, why might you encourage someone to fish a spring creek?*

On the other side of things, I would encourage anyone that has a basic grasp of casting a fly rod and knowledge of fly fishing to at least try fishing on a spring creek. I guess it's like anything else, you rarely can judge what it's like without actually trying it out. How do you know whether you like it or not if you don't do it?

*What would be your favorite five spring creeks in Montana?*
Armstrong, Depuy's, Ben Hart, Thompson, and Big Spring.

**Quick-Glance Summary:**

Spring creeks normally have consistent flow and temp at the source

Slow down and observe

Know your hatches

Exact imitation is helpful but not crucial

Softer, slower rod

Fluorocarbon tippet material

Walk the banks, from a distance, before casting

Be courteous to other anglers

# Intimate Settings

## Small Streams Offer
## Big Rewards

No lie: the biggest fish I caught last summer, a whopper brown trout pushing 24 inches, came out from the smallest body of water I fished all year, a tiny creek that fed into a fairly popular, floatable river. It was August, and the fish had likely pushed up into the yard-wide creek to access cooler water. Snagged my hopper pattern not once, but twice, in the grass before finally landing it on the stream—a sudden surge of current and a huge white mouth, then I was tied to a hog.

### Just how small is too small a creek to fish?

Having caught fish in streams barely deep enough to cover a trout's back, I don't think there exists a stream too small to fish. No matter where fish live, they need the same three things: food, oxygenated water, and cover. If they can find these three things, they don't care if they're living in a "Blue Ribbon" magazine-whored river, or some unnamed feeder stream.

As a young angler, no stream was too small for my taste. I used to spend a lot of time in the backcountry, hiking into rarely accessed lakes and streams. Basically, my theory was: He who walked the farthest would find the biggest fish. This of course was not always true, as my brother Carl was fond of reminding me when he returned from a night on the Madison battling bruiser browns and I came back from a small stream up the Gallatin with tales of 10-inchers. Often, I learned, high-country fish live within a shorter growing season than do the big river fish. Without fail, though, I found solitude, great country, and beautiful, hungry, wild fish, such as Yellowstone cutthroats, usually in their native environment.

## Are the hatches any different?

One of the fascinating things about small streams is that they are often miniature versions of the big rivers, complete with similar bug life and hatch calendar. However, as one climbs in altitude, one finds the hatch calendar pushed back a few weeks. The green drake hatch, for instance, might occur in late June on the Big Hole, but not until late July on some of the higher elevation streams around there, that I won't name for fear of serious retribution by the hands of locals.

On most small streams, spring creeks excluded (see next chapter for information), bug life is relatively simple to imitate. On the Missouri River, I might carry three sizes and over a dozen different patterns of pale morning dun mayfly imitations; on a small tributary, though, like Little Prickly Pear, I can likely get by with one or two general PMDS. The same goes for caddis and stoneflies—just a couple of patterns, such as elk hairs and stimulators, are needed—which small-stream trout love twitched. Additionally, because branches and bushes often hang over small streams, small water trout are often suckers for a terrestrial imitation, such as an ant or a beetle. In recent years, I've had some fantastic fishing near Big Sky, Montana, on small waters during the August spruce moth event.

## Do I need to be more of a predator?

The answer, as always, is *yes!* At least if I want to catch more fish, I do. This means wearing drab, even camouflaged clothing, and staying low against the horizon as much as possible. Also, I try not to wade in the water if conditions allow; I try to tiptoe up the bank with the softest steps possible. Years of experience have taught me that it's noise first, not visual disturbances, that spook fish. Finally, generally when fishing small streams, I make my way up the creek so as not to send every spooked fish downstream to spook the others, but there are some exceptions to this rule, such as when conditions allow me to feed a fly a long ways downstream from a hidden position. When fishing small streams, I find constant reminders of my own inability to remain in stealth mode: water stirred by a fleeing fish, a wake or a shadow moving upstream away from my pounding feet.

## What about seasonal considerations? When streams are low and warm?

For much of this discussion so far, I've concentrated on higher-elevation small streams, but there are many incredible small streams that run through the lower elevations, too. As the summer progresses, it's important to step back and look at the thermal conditions of all small streams, to decide whether fishing them is good for the resource.

Nerdy as it sounds, I often carry a thermometer with me in my vest so that I can check to make sure water temps aren't creeping up into the danger zone for fish. When water reaches the high 60s, you should back off the fish, at least during the warm hours of the day, and when it approaches 70, you should skip fishing altogether and go swimming or rafting. Many people think that small streams, because they are thermal refuges for trout, can be fished all the time, no matter what the temperature, but this is not the case. Because they lack the volume of big rivers, small streams often warm up more quickly than big rivers. What's more, when fish have fled the big rivers for cooler temps upstream, they don't need the additional stress of being caught.

## Can streamers be used on small streams?

Many people wonder if big-river tactics can be applied on small streams, and the answer is almost always "Yes!" In addition to dry flies and nymphs, streamers, for instance, can be fished to astounding ends on small streams, especially for brown trout that love to hug the under-cut banks.

From an upstream position, cast the streamer, a small Woolly Bugger or zonker, down and across the water (let it thwack the water, as fish often strike on instinct!), and make a mend toward the under-cut bank. Slowly, then, with rod tip pointed toward the bank, strip the fly upstream.

Big browns will literally cartwheel out of the water for your fly, which is imitating everything from a cranefly larva to a fleeing min-now. Finally, in the fall, don't forget to try this tactic at the mouths of small streams where browns stage before spawning.

## Will my 9-foot five-weight work?

Frankly, any rod will work for fishing small streams. Sure, your 9-foot five-weight will work. So will an eight-weight. But you'll have much more fun fishing with a shorter, lighter rod such as an 8-foot three-weight, or something along those lines. The weight of the rod you fish has almost no bearing on the size of fish you can land with said rod. I've caught five-pound brown trout on spring creeks with a zero-weight rod before. However, I will leave you with one note of caution regarding rods for small stream fishing:

There are loads of great small-stream buddies out there, but I rec-ommend something middle of the road as far as expense is concerned, since you'll likely be tromping in some pretty rough country with this little rod, busting through brush, etc.

## What's all this talk about Tenkara? That's just a fad, isn't it?

All the talk about Tenkara rods is just that: talk. The principle devolved from dapping (sneaking along the bank, then dangling the fly over the water without a cast, and letting it touch the water right over a fish's nose), which can clearly be accomplished with a tradi-tional rod and reel.

### What about private property issues?

No matter where you choose to fish small streams, private property issues will come into play. In Montana, for instance, once an angler accesses a navigable stream from a legal access, he may go where he wants so long as he stays below the high-water mark. Here, "navigable" is the operative word, as some streams do not look "navigable" in the late summer despite being floatable in June. To be safe and respectful, always ask nearby property owners if you are confused. Nine out of ten folks will happily oblige your inquiry, maybe even give you some advice or directions to the best hole.

However, keep in mind that Montana's stream access law does not apply in Wyoming and Colorado, where landowners can actually own the streambed. Here, rod fees and trout clubs are beginning to become the norm—except in the high country where National Forest land allows everyone (even cows!) access.

### What are the top five things to consider when fishing small streams?

Over the years in guiding, I've found that many Midwesterners come to the West with a predetermined bias against the big rivers, and stick to their comfort zone of 30- to 40-foot-wide streams. Their flies get lost out on the big currents, they say, and there are too many boats and people around. In some ways, they're right, but really, big rivers are just small rivers magnified, and the same fishing principles apply in both venues.

So, whether fishing a big river but thinking about it as a small, or actually plying small waters, this checklist of five things is worth keeping in mind:

- ACCESS: Do I have permission, either by law or landowner, to be where I am? And, if I do, where does this access run out? At the bridge, at the fence line? Below the National Forest boundary? Knowingly or unknowingly, I hate to trespass. There's just too much good public water out there to justify it, as well as too many kind landowners who allow permission to their land.

- FLIES AND GEAR: Normally, you don't need many flies to embark on a small stream mission. I keep a "pocket box" handy, a small container loaded with just enough flies to get me through a day trip to a creek, something I can fit in the breast pocket of my fishing shirt. The box is filled with "generals," such as elk-hair caddis, leggy stimulators, Royal Wulffs, and the like, as well as a few olive Woolly Buggers and prince nymphs of various sizes, maybe a San Juan worm or two. Most small mountain streams won't hold very discriminating fish, but if I do find a fish that won't take one of my "usual suspects," I trim it down in size, reduce its profile a little, and that usually does the trick. A Parachute Adams stripped of its hackle, for instance, can turn into a deadly "emerger" when needed. With this "pocket box," a pair of hemostats, nippers, and another pocketful of tippet, I'm set to go.

- WILD COUNTRY: While much of the small-stream fishing I do occurs out in a farmer's field within sight of the barn, I often head into the high country, too, and try to put some good distance between myself and the truck before I start fishing. In these situations it's easy to forget that I'm in wild country— God forbid out of cellphone range! When wading across the slick rocks, I try to remind myself often: Be careful, you're a long way from a hospital, and there's no one around to carry you to the truck. Also, I make sure to tell someone—never another angler, though!—where I've gone, so that if I come up missing they know where to look. And finally, I always pack enough food and water to get me through the day, as well as a good raincoat and matches.

- TWITCHY-TWITCHY: True, you should relax when fishing, but that doesn't mean you can't twitch—the fly, that is! Over the years I've found that small-stream trout LOVE a fly with movement. So, raise your rod high, lift your leader off the water, and make that caddis pattern dance!

- KEEP YOUR FEET MOVING AND YOUR MOUTH SHUT: One of the most magical things about fishing, to my mind at least, is the possibility of discovering an untouched or under-fished stream, or even just a hidden run or hole on that stream. Or—and this is most likely—finding that hole that lights up at just the right time of day during a morning Trico spinner fall or an evening caddis emergence. True, there isn't much water in the West that hasn't been fished at some point or another over the years. But the farther one walks upstream, away from roads and cars, the more likely one is of finding that Shangri-la. And when you do find it, hoard it like a smart dog holds a map to a buried bone!

# Expert Advice: Craig Matthews

## Small Stream Angling:
## Sweating the Small Stuff

*Blue Ribbon Flies*
West Yellowstone, Montana
www.blueribbonflies.com

Craig began tying flies at age six with gull and starling feathers. Eventually his love of fly fishing brought him to West Yellowstone, where his first group of angling partners reads like a "who's who" of celebrities— Charlie Brooks, Bud Lilly, Dan Bailey, Dick McGuire, Pat Barnes, and many others. Matthews' angling style and conservation-minded philosophy were molded by his time spent with these greats. The angling influences in Craig's life encouraged him to explore small streams, and when Matthews mentioned to Charlie Brooks that he would try to fish all the creeks in the Yellowstone area, Brooks replied with, "Kid, you can't fish them all, even in two lifetimes!" Since then for the sake of fun and exploration, Matthews is still trying to fish them all. Along with Yvon Chouinard, founder of Patagonia Inc. Craig started 1% for the Planet Club, an alliance of businesses that contribute at least 1 percent of their annual revenues to groups on a list of researched and approved environmental organizations. He is the author of *Western Fly-Fishing Strategies* and the coauthor of *The Yellowstone Fly-Fishing Guide, Fishing Yellowstone Hatches, Fly Patterns of Yellowstone,* and *Fly Fishing the Madison River.* He has narrated and produced three Telly Award-winning DVDs on fly fishing: *Fly Fishing Yellowstone Hatches*, *Fly Tying Yellowstone Hatches*, and *Bone Fishing the Flats*. His latest DVD is *Fly Fishing the Madison River*. Blue Ribbon Flies has been awarded several conservation and environmental awards for helping preserve, protect, and enhance western trout waters for future generations.

*In this chapter we are talking about fishing small streams. Would you say that small-stream angling requires a different mind-set than a larger river?*

Fishing small streams early on taught me the single most important thing a fly fisher can know: the character and quality of streams he fishes. A small stream reads easily, and it tells you what to do when you study it. It can be much more intimate than a huge heavy flowing river.

*Is fishing small streams easier than larger rivers?*

Usually small freestone streams are easier to fish than larger water. They are easy to wade, the fish might be less selective, and the water is easier to read. However, no single kind of stream in the West holds more secrets, water types, and insect activities yet receives less angling attention than freestone streams. The fact that trout in freestone streams tend to be a bit easier to dupe does not mean you can get away with sloppy presentation or approach. Cover is nearby, and if you spook a fish, they'll be down for the day.

*What may be the first thing an angler thinks about when approaching a small stream?*

When most anglers first see small freestone streams, they usually appear too fast and shallow to hold any significant trout. Often though, these busy mountain streams have sections of meadow water, a beaver dam or two along their course, and good pockets and runs if the angler is willing to walk and explore.

*If an angler is heading out or standing at a small stream, how should they begin their fishing?*

I never arrive on the stream until noon. On this water type the water temps are so low insect emergences and dry-fly activity seldom happen before then. Arriving at a small freestoner, I usually sit on the bank for a few minutes and ready my gear—tying on tippet and organizing my equipment for the day. I will check streamside vegetation for any aquatic insects like mayflies, caddisflies, or stoneflies that might have emerged and tie on an imitation. I do what the stream tells me to do by checking for insects.

*Do you have a preferred method, be it fishing dries, streamers, or nymphs?*

I like to fish dry flies on freestone waters. The fish usually rise immediately to most any high floating imitation if they are in the mood. But freestone waters are somewhat unpredictable due to cold water and late runoff, as most originate high in the mountains. Their insect emergences are always unpredictable, so anglers should expect them later than those on larger lower-elevation rivers. This unpredictability makes it tough to plan what type of fishing you might have. You should always be prepared for almost anything.

*Many times you will find yourself in tight quarters; how would you adjust your casting to keep from hanging up on trees, willows, or other things?*

I find I use two methods to deliver flies to fish on freestone waters when obstructions behind threaten. The first is a simple roll cast. Another effective presentation is that of dapping—sneaking along the bank, keeping a low profile. Look for the outside, the deepest part of a meander. Without casting, I will dap my leader, tippet, and fly on the water in front of rising trout just off the end of my rod. I use streamside vegetation, high banks, and any cover to conceal my approach.

*You've mentioned there is no need to begin to fish much earlier than noon. What about the pace at which you fish or cover water?*

I think it is often best to cover a lot of ground to find the prime pockets, pools, and meadow stretches present on many freestone streams. Otherwise much freestone water is barren of all but the smallest trout. If the stream is moving fast and offers little or no security or protection from the current, I keep moving until I find better holding water.

*What would be some specific bits of advice for a beginner on a small freestone?*

Take a good selection of high-floating dry flies for searching freestone waters, also a selection of small streamers and general nymphs that imitate the caddis, mayflies, and stoneflies I might expect to find. Bring a few dry imitations of these insects and a terrestrial selection too. A pair of hippers or wet wading shoes is usually adequate.

Cover lots of ground and cast to each good-looking hold only once or twice before moving as trout usually respond on your first cast. Always work upstream and use short casts.

*What about advice for experienced anglers?*

Far too few experienced anglers visiting the West spend time exploring and learning smaller freestone waters. They are full of surprises—fine insect emergences bringing lovely rises of wild trout with few, if any, other anglers. Quite often these busy little mountain streams have sections of meadow water and beaver dams along them. On such stretches the character of the stream can change from mountain freestone to a smooth spring creek or slough or pond requiring changes in strategies and techniques. I always fish upstream. I present my casts on a short slack-line cast and dead-drift it whether fishing a nymph or dry fly. I seldom wade unless to cross here and there for a better cast when I sneak up on a pool, pocket, or overhang. If I'm fishing to rising trout, those working emerging caddis or mayflies, I position myself about 15 feet below a rising fish. I determine what the trout is rising to and present a pinpoint cast. Remember that trout rise in very narrow feeding lanes on freestone waters and will not move for naturals or artificials outside these lanes.

*Do you often fish streamers?*

I find freestone streams can be fished effectively with small streamers fished straight upstream, using either a dead drift or a rapid, jerky retrieve. I fish streamers that imitate sculpins and other bait fish that inhabit freestone waters like juvenile whitefish patterns and small imitations of rainbow and cutthroat trout.

*It sounds like many of the streams require a little extra effort to fish. What are some precautions or problems anglers might face?*

Always carry bear spray, also known as pepper spray, and be aware of bears at all times. Being aware of bears means keep an eye out, try to fish with someone, or if alone make noise and exercise caution. Never drink from the small streams, all host Giardia, known as beaver fever, so bring along a filter or clean drinking water. You must cover a lot of water using short casts. The better fish will hold where they are expected: in the riffles and runs, pockets and pools, under overhangs and sweepers. Remember that these waters fish best late in the season; July, August, and early September are best. Late, cold runoff makes for unpredictable fishing early in the season. Too, the water temps are cold early in the day and fall off early in the evening so midday angling is always best. Many anglers are not in good physical condition to tackle the rigors of high elevation and tough terrain to fish these waters. Get in shape!

*You've mentioned that anglers need to bring a wide array of flies. What are some of your favorite flies to fish freestone waters?*

I like fishing our Sparkle Dun pattern to imitate mayfly emergences like pale morning duns, Baetis, Gray and Green Drakes, and any other mayflies emerging on freestone waters. These flies float well, are durable, and imitate any and all mayflies tied in the proper sizes and colors. For caddis I prefer our X2 or standard X Caddis. The same here as above, these flies float well, are durable and very effective, and easy to tie. For terrestrials I like our Chaos Hopper, Blue Ribbon Foam Beetle, Zelon and Racy Flying Ants, X Crickets, and Yellowstone Bees.

*Is matching the hatch critical when fishing small creeks?*

When trout are rising to a specific insect activity such as a pale morning dun hatch or caddis emergence, I find it best to go with a fly that imitates that insect. This is why I prefer Sparkle Duns and X Caddis; they imitate an impaired mayfly or caddisfly, a stage that trout recognize and are comfortable taking whether on a freestone or spring creek.

For trout rising to land-borne insects like grasshoppers and beetles, I find exact imitation not near as critical due to size variations in both insects, which might be present in the drift on a freestone stream.

*How do you suggest anglers fish to rising trout in this smaller setting?*

You will find several fish rising in a pool or run during mayfly or caddis hatches. Trout in freestone streams do not have the luxury of heavy or long-lasting emergences as do trout in larger streams or spring creeks, so they tend to be a bit greedier. Get as close to feeding trout as you can so you can see him take your fly. If a smaller trout should take it, let him spit it out without hooking him and disturbing the pool. I recall many times allowing small trout to race in and take my offering then reject it. I then allow the fly to float clear of the smaller fish before re-casting it, hopefully to a larger trout.

*Do you suggest a certain rod or rod size for these lesser-size waters?*

I like a rod that can quickly turn over a leader and fly whether it be a large grasshopper pattern, high floating Royal Wulff, or #16 pale morning sparkle dun. My favorite tool is a 9-foot five-weight Winston B2X.

*When it comes to leaders and tippets, what sort of adjustments or preferences do you take?*

I like a 9-foot 4X leader to start. Usually this leader suffices for nearly all freestone fishing. When I come upon a meadow section with trout rising selectively to say a #20 Baetis mayfly, I will put on a 2- to 3-foot section of 5X, sometimes even 6X tippet.

*Often times fishing smaller creeks is a great way to get away from the crowds. What might you suggest when you encounter another angler?*

A spooked fish on a freestone stream won't rise again for some time. Once a fish is hooked and played in the pool, the rest are alerted and spooked and will not rise again. If you encounter another angler, ask him or her what direction they are fishing. If you are following behind, it is best to leave and head to another part of the stream.

*Related to seeing other anglers on the water, you are very involved in conservation. How might your personal business philosophy be fitting for small streams?*

Small streams can't handle the angling pressure of larger rivers. So when a business makes a living from a healthy environment such as clean water and air and healthy wild trout populations, that business must give something back to continue that healthy business cycle; sort of like an earth tax. This is the reason our business gives back over 1 percent of our *gross* sales to conservation and environmental causes through the 1% for the Planet Club. This ensures that all future generations might fish and enjoy wild places and wild fishes!

**Quick-Glance Summary:**

Know the character and quality of the water

Small streams hold many secrets

Midday fishing is usually best

Learn the roll cast

Always cast upstream

Use high floating dry flies

Get in shape!

Start with 9-foot 4X

# Chapter Nine

# Self-Reflection

## Questions to Ask Yourself When Fishing

### How do I approach the stream?

In today's run-and-gun fishing world, where fly shops post up-to-the-minute Twitter reports that tell the angler what fly to fish, where to fish it, and what size fish to expect as a result, it's easy to forget that the root, and perhaps purpose, of the sport lies in observation.

To wit, approach the stream as undetectably as possible. This process of becoming invisible begins long before the angler reaches the stream. Remember, "presentation" includes everything from "the costume to the cast," so dress in clothes that will match the color of your surrounding environs. As you make your way toward your desired starting point, try to stay out of the water if at all possible. Walk on the softest ground you can find, and if you must walk on gravel or cobbles, walk wide of your intended stopping spot, and creep your way to the water.

Over the years, while watching wade fishermen on guide trips, I've determined that it's the approach of the fisherman on a run that largely determines his success—not necessarily the cast or even the fly. If you have ever watched a heron walk, you've no doubt noticed that they lift one foot high up out of the water before moving it, set that first foot down, then move their second foot. This process creates very little, if any, wake on the water, and causes few vibrations to resound through the water into nearby fishes' lateral lines.

### Did I survey the situation?

After walking like a heron to your spot, once you get to where you're going, sit and watch awhile. Observe the bug life on the water and in the air. If you can't see any airborne or water-bound bugs, check nearby spider webs and the foam of the back-eddies. Then look for feeding fish, both on the surface and in the water column—flashes and boils of water can indicate fish feeding on nymphs or chasing minnows. Consider the time of day and the water temperature—are you too early for a peak-activity period, or too late? Should you be anticipating a hatch with an emerger or backing one up with a cripple or pork chop?

If you're an experienced angler, you may have already calculated answers to the aforementioned questions in your head, and be anticipating action on a given fly in a given spot. That you have calculated your 20-year-deep fishing logs with the current stream-flow temperature and moon phase to determine that a yellow sally stonefly hatch will commence in fifteen minutes is all well and good, so long as you remember to fully expect the unexpected while you're on the stream.

### Have I fished from "top to bottom"?

If a hole or a run looks productive, meaning it contains good holding water, a hatch is coming off, etc., and you have fished it without success, you should ask yourself: Have I fished from top to bottom?

There are many ways to "dissect" a run, to ensure that you have thoroughly delved its waters.

Usually, I begin by fishing a hole in the least obtrusive way possible: with a dead-drifted dry fly. With multiple casts, I'll try to cover the water with a fan-shaped pattern, moving upstream as I go, getting the longest drifts possible.

If this approach yields no results, I'll change flies at the top of the run to a dry fly I can fish actively, a small caddis, medium-size stonefly, or large hopper that I can fish "on the twitch." Casting down and across the stream, I'll raise my rod tip and wiggle it, to

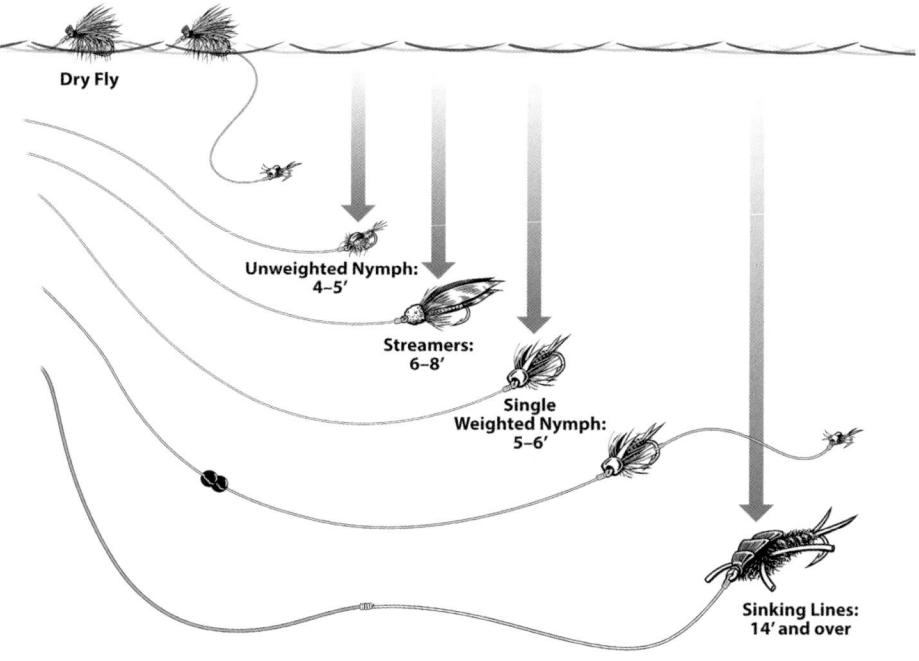

**Dry Fly**

**Unweighted Nymph:**
**4–5′**

**Streamers:**
**6–8′**

**Single**
**Weighted Nymph:**
**5–6′**

**Sinking Lines:**
**14′ and over**

skate the fly across the current, a tactic that often triggers the largest fish in a run.

If I still haven't cracked the code, I'll do one of two things: move on to the next good run, or rig to fish with nymphs. If my targeted holding water is 1 to 3 feet deep, I'll likely tie a dropper nymph onto a large dry fly and explore the water that way. But if my targeted holding water is 3 to 9 feet deep, I'll rig with a full-on, double-nymph indicator rig. As with the first dry fly, I'll fish upstream, quartering across to get a nice long dead drift—but I'll also be sure to let the flies swing out at the end of each drift.

When fishing a run "from top to bottom," it's important to give fish as many different looks as possible: top-water options, deep options, dead-drifted options, swinging options, twitched options. To wit, when I get to the top of the run again with my less-than-successful nymphs, I'll switch to a streamer, or maybe two streamers of different colors, and strip them through the run.

Whatever works in Run #1 tactic-wise will likely work just upstream or down.

## What about other anglers? Is my etiquette appropriate?

Over the years, I have found that "The Golden Rule" doesn't always work when applied to the fly-fishing world. "Treat others as you would like to be treated" often devolves into "Treat others as you wouldn't mind being treated under less-than-desirable circumstances."

When I was growing up, I was always told to yield to the upstream angler when wade fishing, but that assumed that people generally waded upstream. Nowadays, if I'm wading upstream and spot another angler farther up the creek than me, I either turn around, head back to the car, and find another spot, or get on the bank, get wide of the stream, and approach the other angler courteously, letting him know that I'll be walking *at least* three bends

upstream before beginning to fish. A kind-spoken, "How's the fishing?" will usually elicit an answer that tells you whether the angler wants to talk. If the dude drops his head to the water and grumbles, then I just keep walking, but if the guy perks up and says, "They're crushing a size 12 orange Humpy," then I'll stay and chat for a while. The river is a magical place, and sometimes surprisingly important encounters occur there.

Above all, it's important to remember why most people go fishing: to be alone. In recent years, with Facebook and web-madness, the culture of fly fishing has become inundated with very social hardcore "bro-bras"—this is fine. No one person or set of ideals owns the resource—just keep in mind that not only curmudgeons like a little peace and quiet while on the stream.

While drift-fishing, an altogether different set of "guidelines" applies, and each river has its own particular ethic. On the Missouri River, for instance, multiple guide boats will often "dock up" together during high-water when fish are concentrated in several runs per float, waiting for a chance to fish the same run. It's nothing to see four or five boats idling beside "The Bullpen" or another such hole—the boats will take their turns running the seam and, hook up or not, often row back upstream in the slack water so that they can run the same seam again. In August, however, when the fish have spread out river-wide and aren't so concentrated, this kind of gang mentality is generally frowned upon.

Furthermore, we guides should always keep in mind that we are stewards of the resource who represent the industry. For many reasons—some shabby, some solid—guides get a fairly bad rap. Some guides are loud, obnoxious, discourteous on the water, and they do seem to be everywhere. Many of their clients also seem to catch a lot of fish, which doesn't always sit well with other anglers. However, most guides I know pick up trash each day on the river, happily share effective flies with other anglers, have helped keep floaters safe by ensuring proper river-channel navigation—heck, many guides I know have literally saved other floaters' (dogs included!) lives!

If you are ever confused, look to these guidelines:

- Floating anglers should yield to bank and wade fishermen.
- Wade fishermen should yield to boats when there is only one navigable channel.
- Drift anglers should never pass another boat to cut in on water being fished.
- Avoid wading in spawning areas.
- Pick up trash, even if it's not yours.
- Motorboats: no wakes please.
- Keep access points and ramps open by launching boats quickly.
- Conserve the resource. Know the fishing regulations.
- Do not trespass on private land.
- Don't let your actions affect someone else's fishing pleasure. Treat everyone as you would like to be treated, but understand that they may not share your sense of ethics.

### If I am releasing fish, am I doing it with the fish in mind?

The most consistent argument I hear from old-timers against guides is not really an argument but an unsubstantiated assertion: Guides are the reason there aren't any more fish! Granted, most of said old-timers are Royal Coachman–slinging sixty-somethings who don't understand why they can no longer drive to the nearest bridge on the Yellowstone, drag a dry fly through a run on 2X, and catch a 20-inch brown trout. They simply haven't evolved to the current demands of today's trout. Face it, you wouldn't walk into a bar, ask a pretty girl, "What's your sign?" and expect any measure of success, would you?

That said, one thing that guides are guilty of is handling a lot of fish. The average guide releases thousands of fish in a given year, and not all these fish make it. Either they are dropped on the bottom of

the boat after being mishandled by a client for a photo or held out of the water too long for a photo. If you're going to take a picture of a fish that you intend to release, you need to own up to your priorities: Do you want a good photo, or do you want the fish to survive?

Those big, rubber basket nets are essential to good photography, because they allow fish to revive themselves while awaiting their "moment of fame." Wet your hands, cradle the fish gently in your hands, and—*over the net or the water*—hold it toward the camera. Another rule: If it flops, let it drop; it should either end up back in the water or in the net. I've seen too many death-grip fish pictures over the years caused by an angler trying to tightly grip a slippery fish.

# Expert Advice: Robin Cunningham

## Prospecting and Fishing
## New Water for the First Time

*Headwaters Guide Service*
*Executive Director of The Fishing Outfitters Association of Montana*
Gallatin Gateway, Montana
www.headwatersguideservice.com

Robin came to Montana during the first boom in the 1970s, but his trips to the state began way before his zip code became Montanan. Having grown up and fished in the Midwest, Robin would often venture to Montana to fish new and unknown waters. His early days in Montana found Robin camping beside the road or a river, cooking his dinner over a camp stove while searching out his next fishing adventure—perhaps living a life of envy for any serious fly fisher. During that time Robin clearly discovered some new waters for him and for his angling friends as fly fishing in Montana was not an everyday pastime as it is now. His passion for discovering new water eventually led him to Montana's Gallatin Valley, where he's called home for nearly forty years. After a substantial time prospecting the waters in the area, Robin quickly learned he had a knack for teaching anglers and enjoyed the relationships built while guiding. In time Robin has established himself as one of the more well-known guides and outfitters in an area of Montana that has the highest per capita of guides and outfitters in the state. These days Robin enjoys fishing an old regular beat as much as he loves fishing a piece of water for the first time.

*We are going to talk about prospecting new water. How would you define prospecting?*

When I first came to Montana, you could read about and drive to, park at, and fish the big-name rivers such as the Yellowstone and Madison. So you got your bearings by heading toward the big-name rivers. But along the way you would see lots and lots of little creeks, side channels, pieces of water that made you go, "Hmmmm." I was very enthusiastic and I would try everything. And area-wise, because I was based in the Gallatin Valley, I began to look at other places to fish like east of us toward the Bighorn and west to the Clark Fork. I would focus on getting to those rivers and those major towns—there wasn't any specific plan, it was just where do you want to go next. Back then, especially on the smaller waters near the major rivers and towns, it was all word of mouth and rumor. You would drive around and drive around, see something that looked interesting, and ask for permission for things that looked extra-special!

*Did you ever take into account time of year?*

Certainly. One of the trips I wanted to do originally was fish salmon flies all across the state. I knew that would be a great way to learn all of the major waters and the smaller ones. Start with the Blackfoot and Rock Creek and finish on the upper Yellowstone and then into Yellowstone National Park.

*When you were new to the state, how did you learn about all the various waters without feeling overwhelmed with options?*

I did a lot of reading. I also asked a lot of questions. For Colorado waters back then it was Gierach, for Montana it was Bud Lilly. You could meet Bud Lilly and it was great because you could go to his shop and talk to him or his staff and really learn where to go. But a great resource was Curt Thompson's book *Floating Montana*. This guy floated every river in the state and compiled quite the volume. And of course Charlie Brooks's books and as a person, I knew him and he was always eager to share information.

*Would you say anglers today have an easier time prospecting new water to fish?*

Actually, I think it is harder. Because there is much more information out there and all that information cuts down on the curiosity factor. When you can Google-up any stretch of river or find a magazine or find a website that depicts a given stretch of river. A lot of the charm has been bled out of finding new water. Because now it is all sort of "been there-done that," which takes away the mystique of what used to be the "I don't know, I've never been" of many shops and experts. The mystery inspires one to want to go and check it out.

*So you mean it is harder to find those newer waters?*

Newer waters for sure. But for me and for a lot of anglers it is the difference of Lewis and Clark and the geographic survey—there's more to explore individually but certainly less to discover. All of this information can sometimes be more of impediment.

*So, whatever happened to packing up the truck and "just going"?*

Good point.

*What about issues of access?*

When I first came to Montana, I met a lot of Montanans because I was asking for permission to use their land to access rivers. Shortly after I moved here and the stream access law became what it is today, well, every bridge became an access point. That made a lot of water more accessible, but boy it created a whole new plethora of waters to explore and that was exciting. With the passage of the new law, which allowed anglers to basically stay in the streambed once accessed legally, it made prospecting for new water that much more challenging and enjoyable. Before in Colorado floating was particularly difficult because you could not anchor or place the boat on shore in many areas. In Montana being able to go anywhere via a drift boat, canoe, or raft was great.

*Did you do a lot of prospecting through floating?*
Yep. I would put a raft or canoe on top of the camper and head out.

*Did you ever have any conflicts during those first initial years when you did the bulk of your prospecting?*
Actually early on I was doing a lot of walk-wade, so access was attained by knocking on doors, meeting people in bars, and just getting to know Montanans so I might get access to places to fish.

*Once you gained access to a piece of water and you were on the water, explain how what happens next? In other words, how do you break down fishing this new water?*
So if I am standing at a bridge or on the bank, well, a lot of my techniques and suggestions are assuming one has a basis of reading the water. And it is essential to read water not just for the sake of knowing where the fish are but for safety and knowing where to go to avoid trespassing. The first question would be where can I access or can I even get to where I want to go? How far can I get without causing any trouble in trespassing or my own safety? And how might I have to wade somewhere—can I get to the other side, can I get back, can I realistically fish what I want? It really isn't all just fish, it is safety.

*What are the first three things that come to your mind when you are pulling up to an access site?*

Legal access, safety, and finally where to fish.

*What might be some issues of safety that anglers might overlook in their excitement to fish this new piece of water?*

Some questions they need to ask themselves: how deep is the water? How fast is the water? If I go downstream from this spot, how can I get out easily, how can I get across the river easily, and how can I get back to here easily? And the getting back to the access has a lot to do with trespassing.

*You've got legal access and you've studied the safety of the water. You've made your plan and now you are ready to fish. What's next?*

I call what happens next "keeping things in my hip-pocket." I know the places where it is relatively obvious where the fish are based on reading the water. I base that on my previous trout-fishing experience. Then I avoid those spots and put them in my "hip-pocket" for later. Then I really prospect places where whether or not fish are and this is a big question mark. I'm always intrigued by where fish might be. This curiosity is what makes prospecting so much fun.

*How do you determine which places to "prospect" and which places to simply blow-by?*

I bypass really shallow water and really fast water. I know of the places where fish will be in most given trout rivers, so I save those for later— you know, places like a riffle corner, an undercut bank, behind or in front of a rock, etc. Then I look at the water. I look and I look, then I look some more. I watch. I sit down and watch to see what happens in this brand-new water. The typical lies I can pick out right away. My favorite thing to tell people is that avoid getting in the water unless you have to, but again that is why I mention early on to be aware of trespassing. It has happened to me many times and to my clients as well—pulling line out *and* walking to the river and stepping in then a big fish is spooked! The thing to remember is that you do not just dash right in. When people do this, it proves that fish are not always where you think they are, especially in water that you've never fished before.

### What would you term the "other spots" that you search out?

Most anglers know the hot spots and the warm spots, but my curiosity sends me to the "I don't knows" first. And that is what I call them—I am not sure if there are fish there, but I'm going to check it out!

### Now you've watched one of these spots for a while and your curiosity is piqued. How would you begin to fish one of these spots?

First I take into account what may be hatching at the time; however, even if I don't see a fish rise, that doesn't deter me from making a drift in that piece of water. I've caught many big fish during a salmon fly hatch in a spot where I did not have any idea whether there was a fish there, especially a big fish. But most of the general prospecting that people do occurs during a non-hatch period. Remember, keep in mind that I've got in my hip-pocket the fact that I can head back to one of the "hot spots" and most likely catch a fish—that is why the places that are a little mysterious are the most fun for me. This may be the tail of a pool or the outside of a bend, but I always give these a look or a cast.

### What about fly selection?

I observe to see what is happening around me first. I then look to impressionistic flies first, rather than very specific flies. An Adams instead of a Crippled Etha-Wing Half Down Blue Winged Olive. I don't try to match the hatch, I try to use something that is an impression of the hatch. I prospect a lot with attractors. I am a firm believer in my "three to five" theory. Three to five casts, three to five bugs, and most of this from a particular spot for about three to five minutes. That means I would do the "three to five" in a given spot, in one of those "I don't knows," before moving on to the next spot or changing flies. I will always start on the top with a dry. The next few steps are out of necessity, but only if I've had repeated lack of hits in a given spot. But then I will generally go to a dropper nymph before two nymphs fished deep. I will also often prospect with a Woolly Bugger as well. This tactic of changing flies covers the various depths of the water.

*So you would consider yourself fairly mobile while fishing?*
Certainly. Again I've got several places to cast my fly stashed in my "hip-pocket" so I can always put my three to five to use in one of those. It's those unknown spots that keep me moving from one to the next. In general I fish pretty fast, and with my mobility I am always aware of my stance, especially in relation to my backcast. We've all done this, but I can't tell you how many times I get so wired on a new spot and then wham! My first backcast gets snagged in a tree. Depending on where you are standing, it is always good to look behind you. Experts do it all the time, we get excited and bing!

*So when you do something like hook your backcast in a tree, what is the first thing you do? I always look around to see if someone saw me do that!*
I don't care—it happens to all of us. I just make sure it is safe to go and retrieve the fly.

*What about stealth and approach in prospecting?*
Very important. Again, an angler doesn't want to just trounce right into the creek. The classic example I like is the magazine cover image of the angler walking along a high bank with the rod held high, well,

that looks nice but the real prospecting angler is one who is trudging through the bushes, getting his net caught on branches, and is risking tearing his waders as he crawls along the bank.

*How soon would you drastically change the way you are fishing, for example switch from single dry to tandem nymph rig?*

My game is to figure out the water, so I will fish those "I don't know" spots until I know it is dead water. And that entails all methods—nymphs, streamers, dries. Sometimes I look at a big stretch that contains several hot spots, a few possible spots, and lots I don't knows; I will stick with a dry and fish them all. I just enjoy fishing dries more than nymphs or streamers, but I improve my angling ability by trying different methods.

*Would you say that one of the best ways to become a better angler is to fish new water?*

Absolutely. It is a training ground. Going fishing during a hatch can be the simplest fishing—you know the fly, you can see the fish, all you have to do is figure out how to get the two together. Whereas in prospecting new water, you don't know if there are any fish there at all. If there is no hatch, you are not sure what bug to try and you don't know what they are eating. It is all a mystery. Hatches are great, I love them because you have rising fish and it is a whole other way to fish.

*Would you say there is one tactic, be it dries, nymphs, of streamers, to learn where the fish are in a given river or stream?*

There are more fish under the water then there at the top. Plain and simple. But the nice thing about fly fishing is that the angler gets to choose. Is it catching lots of fish or is it fishing a new piece of water? The point of all prospecting is to learn and enjoy. There is a lot to be said for not going right to a hot spot and instead learning something new for yourself, whether it is about the stream or even a new technique. Anglers need to fish at their own pace and break down a stream the way it is enjoyable for them.

**Quick-Glance Summary:**

Get out a map and start looking for water

Be very aware of trespassing and access laws

Safety first

Look and observe before getting in the water

Have thorough knowledge of reading water

Dries, nymphs, and streamers will all work

Save the hot spots for last

Focus on the "I don't knows"

Fish at your own pace

Learn and enjoy

# Chapter Ten

# Everything Else Under the Sun

## Saltwater Angling, Travel, Teaching Kids and Spouses, and More

### Should I carry on or check my rods and gear?

There you are, and we've all been there: you made all your connections, even landed on time, weather forecast is perfect for your trip, and your excitement radiates the baggage claim area. But your bags buck the odds of the airlines and they failed to arrive. This is an awful situation, especially when your luggage contains fishing equipment, and the situation worsens when one's destination is remote and a long way from a fly shop. It's one thing if you're traveling out to

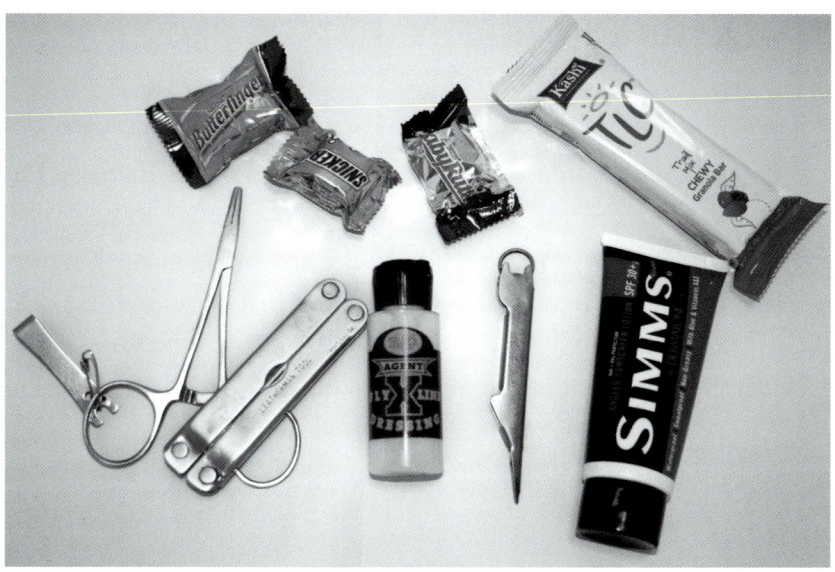

Montana to fish with a guide you've known for years—no worries, they'll have a spare rod for you and there's a fly shop on every corner. However, let's say you've ventured to the Amazon to check peacock bass off your angling bucket list and the airlines lose your gear—not so good.

For a few years after 9/11, some airlines and the Transportation Safety Administration wouldn't allow rod cases as carry-ons. Regulations have since relented, and in recent years I've been able to carry my rods with me on the plane. Depending on where I am going, I use a case that fits multiple rods. I prefer to have my rods, reels, flies, and tackle arrive with me, and check my clothes, journals, etc. Especially if I'm going to the Caribbean, my take is: I can fish in my boxers, but not without my rods.

## What about shipping things to my destination?

Over the years, I've had more and more clients ship their gear to me in a box a week or so before their trip. They get everything together, waders included, and send it UPS to the fly shop or even my house. This seems to work quite well. Some clients, those who fish multiple times a year with me, have even started leaving their gear with me over the season. And I don't mind—I just charge a docking fee: one bottle of Crown Royale per box.

By choosing to ship your gear ahead of time, you always make traveling much easier. As soon as you check your fishing luggage, you are opening up a can of worms. One year I had two clients who'd fish together for years. They missed a connection in Denver and because the airline regulations often require you to travel on the same plane as your bags, one angler made a flight, the other didn't. That meant one angler made it to Montana when he was supposed to . . . the other spent the night near the airport. I caught fish in Montana.

## How do I store my gear for the season?

You know the old saying "Rode hard and put away wet"? Well, fly-fishing gear doesn't hold up too well under such circumstances. Trust me, I've had my share of unfortunate discoveries—the reel seat that has expanded over the winter in the rod case because I failed to fully dry the rod before putting it away; the box of intricately tied mayflies whose hooks rusted because I failed to dry them after a rainy October day; the pair of waders that literally grew mold over the winter while stored in the seatbox of my drift-boat; the list goes on.

It's important to remember that our last fishing days of the year are usually the coldest, and sometimes the wettest, and we're wont to hurry our gear away without much care, so that we can saddle up to the fire or the nearest bar. When putting gear away for the winter, make sure to dry rods and reels with a towel—if you've got some, put a drop of Abu Garcia reel lube in the gears of your reel. If your flies have gotten even damp, take them out of the box and dry them between two paper towels, near a ventilation source.

Hang your waders upside down in a cool, dry place, and store your fishing atlas where no one else can find it.

## How do I teach my partner or kids to fish? Am I good enough?

As you sit sipping some scotch after the season's final excursion, you may think to yourself: This solitary angling is nice, but I would like to have some company next year. Perhaps I'll get my partner a rod and reel for Christmas.

My advice to you here is: proceed slowly. Your partner may enjoy having you away for a few days each month, and she/he may not even like the idea of "standing in a river and waving a dumb stick around in the air," as Norman Maclean once called fly fishing. Also, note whether your relationship is a competitive one. In my experience, a little friendly competition isn't bad on the river, but a little bit more than a little friendly competition can be quite awful.

But you're still determined, you say, and you want to know how to teach your spouse or kids to fish? Quite slowly, and with the utmost patience, stressing that what's most important is not catching fish or even casting competence, but the time spent together away from phones, televisions, offices, cars, buildings, board meetings, errands, appointments . . . did I make my point?

Are you good enough to teach others to fish? Are you patient enough to teach others to fish? I'd argue that the worse you are, the easier it will be to teach, or to learn together. You don't need to be an expert: trust me, it's not always fun. The honest question to ask yourself is, "Can I put my needs below someone else's, allowing them to learn?" Then, pick a stream filled with small dumb cutthroat trout and pretty views nearby; if you're with your spouse, take a picnic and a bottle of wine—you never know what will happen!

### How do I find a good guide?

If you really want to teach your spouse to fish, get someone else to do it: a guide or a course. Hiring a guide or taking a course is a very good idea. This gives an opportunity to improve your skills together and make the outings enjoyable. Just be sure to communicate with the instructor or guide about everyone's expectations for the day. I'm not sure how many times I attempted to teach a thing or two to my significant other before I realized that she always listened to my guide friends better than she listened to me. I remember the first time a guide buddy of mine taught her how to mend.

"Just make a C shape with a your rod tip, and flick the line upstream."

"And that's a mend?" she said.

"Yep, that's a mend."

"Cool," she said, as I sat in the back of the boat shaking my head, counting the dozen or so times I'd tried and failed to explain the mend to her.

The lesson here is simple: The ears of the instructed are open wide when the instruction's not coming from you. So hire someone else to do it, and sit back, enjoy the day, maybe even catch a fish or two.

If you're sold on hiring a guide, there are a few aspects of the transaction worth considering:

1.  Book your guide as far in advance as possible. In the trout fishing world, peak seasons are booked up to twelve months in advance, and this number doubles in the saltwater world. While you may luck out and get a stellar guide who had a recent cancellation or a young up-and-comer who is eager to impress, you may also get the tenth man on the totem pole, or someone an outfitter dragged off a barstool.

2.  If it's fiscally possible and time allows, commit to fishing more days than one. In my experience, it often takes till lunchtime to get in a groove with a client, and it's nice to be able to extend that groove over a period of a few days. By the end of a day's fishing, I can usually accommodate for an angler's "bad casting

habits" with boat position, and can know thoroughly what types of angling they are capable of and prefer, and thus make more informed choices the following day.

3.  Speak with your guide or outfitter before your trip. Let them know what your hopes and preferences are for the day. Do you like to rise early and get a jump on the day? Do you prefer to eat Pop-Tarts in the boat, rather than have the guide grill a fancy lunch? Would you rather catch six fish on a single dry fly than fifty on nymphs? Do you have to be back for dinner reservations at 7? These are all things a good guide can and will accommodate, and you should make sure to communicate your preferences.

4.  It may take years to find your ideal guide. There are many fantastic guides out there, true professionals who take their job as anglers, historians, and stewards of the land quite seriously. But not every guide is right for you. You may be the kind of client who wants just a bit of instruction, and then to be left to your own devices; or you may be the type of client who wants the guide in your ear all day. Whatever your style, there's a guide out there who can match it—it just might take some time to find her or him.

5.  Be a gracious client. The guide/client relationship is just that: a relationship. Ninety percent of the guides out there want to catch fish more than their client does, even though it doesn't always appear as such. If your guide makes a suggestion, try it wholeheartedly. Remember, a guide trip is an investment in your fishing future. During a lull in the action, your guide might teach you a technique today that you successfully apply next season. It's not all about catching fish right now.

    a)  Be a gracious client who tips heavily. Most guides have to cover their shuttle ($20–$50), lunch ($35), flies ($15), and gas. A generous tip for a hard day's work goes a long way to accounting for these costs; if you are ever unsure what to tip, just ask—you'll know if the guide is being honest because you've just spent the entire day with him or her.

## Saltwater fly fishing can seem intimidating. Do most trout anglers have to adjust to the salt game?

Up to this point, I've concentrated almost solely on freshwater trout fishing as it pertains to rivers. And while this type of fishing is what I spend most of my time doing, I absolutely relish the few days of saltwater fly fishing I get to partake in each year.

In my late teens and early twenties, I spent a lot of time at my family's condo near Sanibel Island chasing redfish, jacks, sea-trout, snook, and the occasional tarpon. When I first began plying the salt, I had a fair amount of freshwater angling experience under my belt, but I was totally unprepared for what I was to experience from these fish. I needed a lot more time on the water and a lot more education.

These saltwater fish required much keener eyesight to spot; what's more, they required longer casts through stiffer wind to reach; and finally, they fought harder—even the so-called trash fish—than anything I had ever touched in fresh water.

## Is the cast really that important?

Presentation-wise, the biggest difference between freshwater fly fishing and saltwater fly fishing is the cast. Whereas the river-bound trout angler can get by with a marginal single haul much of the time, the saltwater angler must depend on a well-polished double haul to get the fly through prevailing winds to where it needs to be. This is largely because the trout angler often has the aid of the current to help drift the fly toward the fish, whereas fish in the salt are usually cruising and demand the fly directly in front of their nose. Now, I've caught plenty of red and bonefish with not more than a rod length's worth of line in the water, and sometimes I've seen beginners get lucky and have a fish stumble on their fly five minutes after it was cast, but in general the angler who can't deliver a 75-foot cast into a pretty stiff wind is going to have some struggles in saltwater fishing situations.

### It's like hunting, isn't it?

The reason for this is simple—you get fewer chances at fish in salt water than you do in fresh. Saltwater fly fishing is much more like hunting than most freshwater fly fishing. The saltwater angler is often positioned on the bow of a skiff, a boat that drafts very little water and is poled through the shallow flats by a guide who often stands on a 10-foot-tall platform at the back of the boat. From this vantage point, the guide can spot fish in clear water from an unbelievably great distance away. After spotting the fish, the guide and angler begin their stalk, and when the boat is in position, the angler takes his "shot." Since most fish on the flats feed in water 6 to 18 inches deep, a botched cast is the equivalent of a missed rifle shot that alerts the entire forest to danger. The saltwater angler must always remember that his quarry is much farther down the food chain than the trout. Bonefish, redfish, permit, etc., all lie underneath barracuda and sharks, and even birds of prey in the food chain, versus a large trout, which must only worry about humans and birds of prey.

A great saltwater guide in the Florida Keys, Mike Guerin, always said, "Trout are captives to their home. They really don't want to move. Saltwater fish have to move because their food moves and their prey move."

### What are the species to fish for?

When fishing the salt, most anglers target one of the three glamour species—tarpon, bonefish, or permit—but redfish, snook, and snapper

are equally challenging and rewarding species to chase. While the bonefish offers scintillating runs when hooked, the snook offers a real exciting experience; while the tarpon offers sheer power and size, the mutton snapper offers rarity and brilliance in color; and while the permit offers the ultimate in elusiveness, the redfish offers the precise opposite, as well as strength in flight. In short, there are half a dozen coveted saltwater species to fish for on the flats alone, and they're all worth catching.

## How do I know where to fish?

How do you know where to fish in the salt water? Simply put: you don't, so you hire a guide. At first, anyway, that's what you do. Saltwater flats guides are masters of knowing where to be when, and they determine this destination based on several variable factors: sunlight, wind direction, and tides.

During my early saltwater years near Sanibel, I was lucky enough to catch a fair amount of redfish while wading on my own, but it wasn't until I began taking trips with Mike Rher that I truly understood the mystery of saltwater fly fishing. Mike is a flats fly fishing pioneer who has guided many anglers, including his wife, Joyce, to several saltwater records. After fishing several times with Mike did I understand redfish, and a couple years later, the amazing tarpon.

So, to reiterate: hire a guide. But if you can't afford one, you still have a few plays. You can always walk the beach with a rod rigged and cast into the breaking waves for sea-trout and snook. I've taken some monsters this way. A simple Clouser or Deceiver is all you need to fool these fish, which feed mostly on minnows. Look for seagulls and other birds dive-bombing the water, pushing bait. Sometimes the moving bait will produce a subtle change in the texture of the water, and other times the surface of the sea will literally be boiling with food. Needless to say, it's a visceral experience to fish in such conditions.

If you're determined to try to catch a redfish or bonefish on foot, you're best off searching a flat on an outgoing tide. Bones, permit, and redfish arrive on flats in search of minnows, shrimp, and crabs, which they root out of the soft bottom with their stout noses and crush with their incredibly tough jaws. In general, on the flats of the Gulf and the Florida Keys, because of depth and type of bottom (often covered with turtle grass), wade fishing solo is a difficult proposition. I know of a few maniacs who have had success wade fishing the Keys, among them angling poet and author Chris Dombrowski who, while plying the flats off Long Key, used to drag with him a ten-gallon bucket that he would stand on to get a better view of incoming or tailing fish. Tourists always took photos of Chris standing on his bucket waving his "stick." Most days Chris got the last laugh because he usually caught fish.

Down in the Caribbean, exotic places like the Bahamas, Honduras, or Belize where big schools of bonefish frequently cross white sand expanses, wade fishing success is a more reasonable expectation. Under these conditions, fish "show" themselves much more regularly, and the angler walking a beach with an eight-weight in one hand and a Kalik beer in the other can expect to have shots at schools, or bigger singles, "pushing water," or tailing near the mangroves, respectively.

### Will my 9-foot five-weight work?

While I am certain that many flats-going saltwater species have been caught on trout rods, I wouldn't recommend taking your freshwater outfit down to the salt. For one, the elements of salt and sand are much tougher on reels and line, which is why companies make saltwater reels, which are machined to take more of a bruising. Additionally, saltwater fish make incredibly valiant, surging runs, the power of which could easily break a light rod.

## What special tackle do I need?

If you're ready to commit to a saltwater venture, you'll need to make sure you have a few special tackle items, the first of which is two great pairs of polarized sunglasses. Since seeing fish is the number one priority in salt water, your optics must be top-notch. It's worth owning one pair of glasses with amber lenses for sunny or partly cloudy days, and another pair of glasses with yellow- or rose-colored lenses for darker days. Second, you'll need some loose-fitting quick-dry clothing, preferably in light colors such as sky-blue or tan. Long-sleeved shirts and pants are a must, as is a Buff or sun gaiter, a good hat, wading boots or flats booties, waist-fitting tackle bag to store your flies, fluorocarbon tippets, hemostats, and heavy-duty saltwater pliers.

Also, keep in mind that if you're fishing in a boat, you'll want shoes with non-marking soles so as not to peeve your guide, who will likely prefer you cast barefoot, so as to avoid stepping on your line at the crucial moment. Also, beware of the fact that the sun reflected off the water in lower latitudes is much more intense than even a high-elevation sun. Sunscreen, sunscreen, sunscreen—wear it, so you can keep fishing forever.

Additionally, here are the typical rod and reel combos needed for the corresponding species:

- Seven- and eight-weight rods—bonefish, redfish, sea trout, snook, striper, bluefish
- Nine-weight rod—permit, stripers, false albacore, big jack crevalle
- Ten-weight—smaller tarpon, giant trevally, milkfish, black drum
- Twelve-weight—tarpon, sailfish, and beyond

## What about tides? How important are they, really?

Tides are to salt water what currents are to rivers: everything. Like big-game hunting, saltwater fishing offers little for the sportsman who needs luck to succeed. The stakes are higher and the room for error is slimmer. This is all to say that if you don't know the tides of the area you're fishing, you'll need to get lucky, and you need only watch a shark eviscerate a tired bonefish to know that there ain't much of that around. Local knowledge and tide charts are a must, for both angling success and safety.

# Chapter Eleven

# Websites, Guides, Local and Regional Resources

Since there's a good chance you found out about this book online, I'll assume that you've done some perusing of fly-fishing websites. There are a lot of sites dedicated to fly fishing, and most of them are connected to a shop or an outfitter. Some of these sites do some educating along with their promoting, but I can't point you to them without doing some promoting of my own. I trust you'll find them.

That said, there are many resources out there for the beginning angler, and your local fly shop is resource number one. When I was a youngster in the industry, they used to call guys like me "shop rats" because we were always around asking questions, buying flies two at a time, looking for new secrets from the guides, a hand-me-down streamer, or directions to an under-fished access.

Back then, there seemed to be an over-abundance of crotchety shop owners, guys who might "deign" to give a tip or two but secretly despised their own choice to buy or manage a fly shop. The good news is those days are gone. With the advent of technology in the industry, people have taken note of how truly important a personal connection is. So, before pursuing everything online, make a visit to your local shop, and see what kind of personality it has to offer along with its information.

## Midcurrent

www.midcurrent.com

Kept up by Marshall Cutchin, this site harbors columns on fly-fishing art, photography, gear, techniques, books, flies, knots. Remember the old book, *Everything I Ever Needed to Know I Learned in Kindergarten?* You could safely say the same thing about fly fishing and MidCurrent. It's that thorough, and that substantial, and sets the bar that high.

## The Angler's Tonic

www.anglerstonic.com

This site is maintained by *Fly Rod and Reel* editor Greg Thomas and caters to the hard-but-not-too-hard-core angler, the guy who wants to know as much about where to get a good post-float locally distilled whiskey as he does where to catch the next whopper. On Thomas' site, you'll find game cooking recipes and editorials on why you should disdain farm-raised salmon, tips on how to cast a spey rod, and where not to fish on weekends in Montana. Eclectic and stylish, full of substance, this site is a rarity in the world of fly-fishing shites—er, I mean sites.

## On Fly Fishing

www.onflyfishing.com

Like a gigantic Yellow Pages dedicated to all things fly fishing, this site compiles fishing reports and information from over 100 companies worldwide. Whether you're wondering how to go about booking a trip to New Zealand or when's the best time to fish for rooster-fish in Costa Rica, this phonebook-like website is your base.

## Ozark Angler

www.ozarkangler.com

As a young angler, I would have had a site like this up on my screen 24-7. Of course, there were no websites when I was a young angler, but that's beside the point. When I was starting out in the business, I couldn't tie a fly to save my life, and my friends who tried to teach me just laughed at my ineptitude at the vise. Had the Ozark Angler been around, though, I'd have learned to tie pheasant tails, prince nymphs, and elk hairs overnight. This site is a great resource for the beginning fly tier—worth its weight in gold, or snagged flies, as the case may be.

## The Headhunter

www.headhuntersflyshop.com

Of all the sites, this one, maintained by John Arnold and Mark Raisler, is perhaps one of the most thorough out there on the interwebs. With videos and magazine quality photographs, they cover gear, tactics, fly tying, fishing politics, and more, to create a stunning visual conglomerate of information. Much of their information is Missouri-river specific, but the tactics they address, such as inside-out nymphing or dry-fly mends, can be applied to fishing around the world.

## The Contemporary Sportsman's Guide Shack

www.integrateddigitalpublishing.com/category/blog

An extension of *The Contemporary Sportsman*, an online journal on par with Gray's, this fairly new site couples literate outdoor writing with stunning visuals to create one of the finer reading sites on the market. You might stumble on this site on a whim and find something as humorous as "The Sportsman's Widow," or something as austere as "The Land of Czars," a narrative on fishing Russia.

# Chapter Twelve

# The Fly Fisher's Reading List

**Being a Well-Read Angler Is Just as Important as Being Able to Get It Done on the Stream—You Might Be Able to Walk the Walk, But Can You Talk the Talk?**

To call a book a classic, someone once said, is to ensure that no one will read it. To call a trout stream a classic is to ensure that the throngs will flock to it with guidebook in hand. So what happens when a fly-fishing book is called a classic? Who can say for sure, but the best of them embody the fly-fishing experience so fully that some would rather read them, and live—fish, if you will—through the pages, than stand in flowing water with a fly rod in hand. So does great fishing literature, novels and essays that transcend the sport, actually decrease pressure on our streams? Probably not, but it does afford anglers during cold weather seasons, or the winter of their lives, a subtle way to engage in an act they love. Just as Hemingway's war-injured narrator occupies himself in the recovery ward with daydreams of fishing, so can anglers, through great fishing books, be where they are not: "I had different ways of occupying myself while I lay awake. I would think of a trout stream I had fished along when I was a boy and fish its whole length very carefully in my mind, fishing very carefully under all the logs, all the turns of the bank, the deep holes and the clear shallow stretches, sometimes catching trout and sometimes losing them" *(Now I Lay Me)*.

### A River Runs Through It
Norman Maclean, University of Chicago Press, 1979

At or near the top of nearly every fishing critic's book list is this irreplaceable collection of three novellas, made famous by the film released in 1992, but nominated for the Pulitzer Prize when first published in 1979. Maclean, a University of Chicago Shakespeare professor, wrote the book in his sixties after years of prodding by his children to put down in writing the stories he had told them for years. A writer's writer, Maclean's voice blends eye-bending observation with the poetic sensibility of Wordsworth or Emerson. But he can also be laconic, terse; that the title novella is fully realized in only ninety-two pages is a thing of marvel, and no doubt a result of Maclean's father's strict instruction—in an interview once, Maclean said his father was fond of saying, "My boy, never be too proud to save a single word." Literary or not, Maclean said he was proudest of the book because it was a complete manual on fly fishing, and for years kept letters from anglers who had written to tell him just that. The careful reader will note that it isn't until three-fourths of the book have progressed that a trout is actually *landed* by one of the characters. When Maclean's world of rivers and families is finally distilled into the seminal climactic moment ("I am haunted by waters"), most readers, anglers and non-anglers alike, are left thinking—about not only the final scene but the entire book—*Yes, I wish I'd said it that way.*

### The Longest Silence
Thomas McGuane, Vintage Books, 1999

Thomas McGuane writes as well about fishing as any writer writes about any subject, and *The Longest Silence* is a collection of his nonfiction writings on fishing. His infinitely descript, sometimes hilarious, sometimes erudite prose takes the reader from the small Michigan streams of McGuane's youth to the flats of the Florida Keys, from

British Columbia's steelhead rivers to Russia's Atlantic salmon waters (to give you an idea of McGuane's sense of humor, the latter of these essays is titled "Fly Fishing the Evil Empire"). A former president of the American Rivers conservation group, McGuane writes as effectively about the particulars of tying flies as he does the unfortunate logistics of dewatering practices on Idaho's fabled Henry's Fork. Composed over the course of three decades, these essays will leave even the most ardently observant angler wondering what he or she has been (or hasn't been) looking at all these years. One of those rare writers whose eye for detail is on par with his ability to render those details indelibly to the reader, McGuane's prose on fishing is perhaps the gold standard. The old saying "a day spent reading is a day wasted, but a life spent reading is another story altogether" translates perfectly to McGuane's life if "reading" is replaced with "fishing." His is a voice made wise by waters.

### The River Why

David James Duncan, Sierra Club Books, 1983 (now a Bantam Book)

If Maclean's *A River Runs Through It* is considered a Bible to western anglers, David James Duncan's *The River Why* is their Apocrypha. Irreverent, whimsical, philosophical, and downright hilarious, the book follows Gus Orviston from the waters of his mother's womb to the hidden waters of the Pacific Northwest, where he finds, among other things, love, brief but thorough enlightenment, hatred of how-to angling guides, hangovers, magnificent fish, and his own livable life. Full of blatant and midge-visible literary references, *The River Why's* eclectic blend of Shakespeare and blues singer Taj Mahal, of Izaak Walton and Rumi, has solidified the book a readership that runs the gamut. Duncan's nonfiction books, *River Teeth* and the National Book Award finalist *My Story as Told by Water*, are also high on the list of must read river-born writing.

## Trout Bum or Sex, Death and Fly Fishing

### John Gierach, Fireside Books, 1985 and 1990, respectively

To suggest just one book by former poet turned freelance writer John Gierach is to suggest an angler carry just one pattern in his fly box. Gierach writes for the still-inspired curmudgeons among us, who love to sit around discussing the intricacies of camp coffee or split cane rods as much as they enjoy finding a perfect match to the emerging stage of a pale morning dun. His journeys across the west with fishing partner A.K. Best articulated an entire generation's desire to cut ties, find a decent campsite along a river, and fish until the problems—be they marital, financial, or existential—disappear. Hailing from the semi-arid state of Colorado, Gierach's humor, tested against humidity, passes with flying colors. "Zen and the Art of Nymph Fishing" begins: "Student: 'Master, how does one tell when the trout has taken the fly?' Master: 'The moon is reflected in the still pond, my son.'" Gierach goes on to say that while the man who taught him to nymph-fish isn't a Zen master, an exchange between the two goes something like this: "Student: 'So how do you tell when a fish has taken your nymph?' Master: 'How much did you pay for that rod and reel?'"

## The Angler's Coast

### Russell Chatham, Clark City Press, 1998 (reissue)

Known to most as a painter of striking landscapes, Russell Chatham, called "one of the best angling writers" by the *New York Times*, was angler first and world-class lithographer later, honing his eye for light and landscape on the salmon and steelhead streams of Northern California. The fourteen essays contained in *The Angler's Coast* depict Chatham's angling adventures along the Pacific Coast from Baja, California, to British Columbia, and record an era that is, because of dams and increased fishing pressure, all but memory and lore. Whether shad fishing on the Russian River, or steelheading on the Smith, Chatham sees the art of fishing as a challenge, the mere meeting of which can result in goodness and an increasing of the passionate angler's life.

Some would argue that a selection of the best fly-fishing books would not be complete without any reference to a few "how-to" books. Consciously I've chosen to neglect any how-to books, purely because anglers can spend their own time discovering and learning which how-to books work well for them.

However, there are two books that I feel transcend the average how-to book but are not purely literary. These two books deserve mention purely because they may be a how-to book, but they are merely a how-to book in "sheep's clothing."

## The Dry Fly: New Angles
### Gary La Fontaine, Lyons Press, 2002 (reissue)

This essential and innovative research-based book treads the water between narrative fishing tales and how-to books. Arguably one of the most passionate and experimental fly fishers the West has ever seen, Gary La Fontaine often logged 250 days a year on Montana trout streams, and *The Dry Fly* details the results of and knowledge gained on these excursions. The book's focus is the dry fly, but so much general trout-behavior information is dispensed that the title is a bit of a misnomer; the subtitle "New Angles," however, could not be more fitting. La Fontaine's assertions stem from his laboratory beneath the surface of rivers, into which he scuba-dived and from which he witnessed how trout reacted to different bugs (artificial and natural) at different times of day. Conducted on a relatively scientific level, these experiments drove La Fontaine to fly-tying innovations that seem bafflingly silly to the eye of the angler but perfectly acceptable to the keen eyes of the trout. La Fontaine understood that for a trout to find a fly acceptable, it must first be attracted to a fly, then ultimately triggered by it. Sometimes this equation happens through color, other times through profile, other times through movement, and often all of the above. Fly plates and tying recipes appear in the middle of *The Dry Fly* to give the inspired angler a place to embark on his or her own experimentation. And in the end, La Fontaine isn't just experimenting and relating his results; he is teaching us, as no one before or after, to "think like a fish."

## Presentation
### Gary Borger, Tomorrow River Press, 1995

While Gary La Fontaine's *The Dry Fly* teaches the reader to think like a fish, Gary Borger's *Presentation* teaches the reader to think like a fish's predator. From the book's onset, the reader is instructed to rethink the predator/prey relationship, to eschew the notion of the trout as all-intelligent being sent to earth to baffle angler after angler. Thus, the reader is taught to enter the food chain, to regard the trout's defense mechanisms, and finally to become aware of the trout's field of vision, ability to hear, taste, touch, and smell. These instructions might seem rudimentary in the hands of a lesser author or angler, but Borger, a biologist by trade, delves further into the fish/fisherperson relationship than seems possible. How can you, he asks, invade the fish's world without the fish noticing? And, in time, he answers this question as it pertains to nearly every imaginable angling situation, providing casting techniques, fly-selection suggestions, rod-and-reel selection, and countless other ways to become less detectable to trout. The book is loaded with semi-heroic fishing anecdotes and intricate fish and insect drawings by Borger's son, Jason, also an author and acclaimed fly caster. Comprehensive, knowledgeable, lucid, and straightforward, *Presentation* is perhaps the only how-to book the angler needs on his shelf.

# INDEX